The Spokes

Slump and W

Edited by Ken C

MW00962667

**Published by Spokesman for the
Bertrand Russell Peace Foundation**

Spokesman 102   2009

CONTENTS

Cover: With grateful acknowledgements to Steve Bell

ISSN 1367 7748   Printed by the Russell Press Ltd., Nottingham, UK

ISBN 978 0 85124 761 8

Subscriptions
Institutions £35.00
Individuals £20.00 (UK)
£25.00 (ex UK)

Back issues available on
request

A CIP catalogue record
for this book is available
from the British Library

Published by the
Bertrand Russell Peace
Foundation Ltd.,
Russell House
Bulwell Lane
Nottingham NG6 0BT
England
Tel. 0115 9784504
email:
elfeuro@compuserve.com
www.spokesmanbooks.com
www.russfound.org

Editorial

Slump and War

The election of Barack Obama came as the culmination of a profound surge of optimism in the United States, and of hope against hope in large parts of the rest of the world. Widely detested, the Bush administration was the most unpopular in living memory.

Obama had fought an audacious campaign, calling in question not only the war in Iraq, but the train of events which had brought the United States into contempt all around the world. The American military, far from exercising full spectrum dominance, was arousing full spectrum detestation. Its symbols were Abu Ghraib, Guantanamo Bay, water boarding and extraordinary rendition.

As the American economy raced from recession to slump, Obama's campaign seemed to gather momentum. Earnest crowds of young people were seen on television singing the anthem of Woody Guthrie:

> 'This land is your land, this land is my land,
> from California to New York Island.'

Would that it were so.

This land creaks with every conceivable injustice, with loss and despair, with cruelty, oppression and contempt, by no means all of which have been exported to the numerous theatres of war. If he were bent upon cleansing the Augean Stables, the labours of Obama would be Herculean indeed. And yet, the mobilisation of millions of formerly excluded voters, of the young, the blacks, the many minorities, must now be a moment of hope. They could indeed make light work of removing the accretion of filth from the Bush years and earlier. Will they be allowed to do so? Early signals from those with whom the President Elect is surrounding himself may promote doubt rather than hope. We continually hear the name Clinton. (Two for the price of one, only slightly shop-soiled.)

Certainly, for change to happen in the area of foreign policy, unambiguous leads would be needed from the administration. These may be difficult to secure, but in some areas the Obama team could secure advance quickly.

The abolition of Guantanamo, and the trial or release of its captives would be relatively simple to secure. For justice to be done, it would be necessary to give Guantanamo back to the Cubans, and put its jailors on

> 'Obama's choice of Chief of Staff, Rahm Emanuel, the House Democrat who received the most donations from the financial sector, sends an unmistakably reassuring message to Wall Street. When asked if Obama should be moving quickly to increase taxes on the wealthy, as promised, Emanuel pointedly didn't answer the question.'
>
> *Naomi Klein*

trial for abuse and any other infractions they may have committed. But even short of that, serious progress would be easy to make.

It would be equally easy to outlaw torture in all its forms, although it might be more difficult to persuade people to believe that new decrees on this matter would be observed. We could see the end of extraordinary rendition. The British collaborators must surely be nervous.

Other areas are far more difficult. What will happen in relation to Palestine, for instance? President Carter called the siege of Gaza 'A crime, an atrocity, and an abomination'. But he was not invited to say anything at the Democrats' Convention, unlike another past President. His role was restricted to silently walking-on.

The old regime had pushed hard to secure sanctions against Iran, based on what now appear to be forged documents. The legacy of the Iraqi weapons of mass destruction is difficult to overcome in the United States. Now the International Atomic Energy Agency (IAEA) has gathered evidence that documents describing a secret Iranian nuclear weapons related research programme 'may have been fabricated'. The documents were gathered by US intelligence in 2004 from sources which have not yet been revealed. They mostly consist of electronic files allegedly stolen from a laptop computer, the property of an Iranian researcher. Much of the American push for United Nations sanctions against Iran is based on these documents. Now that the IAEA has evidence of possible fraud in this case, there has been a marked move towards distancing the Agency from these allegations.

The suspect laptop documents include what purport to be technical drawings to redesign the nose cone of the Iranian Shahab-3 ballistic missile, so that it can carry a nuclear warhead. It is also claimed that the documents show studies on the use of high explosive detonators for nuclear weapons, and blueprints of a shaft intended for nuclear testing. All these studies are now described by the IAEA as 'alleged studies'. The Americans claim that the information derives from Kimia Maadan, a company said by the Americans to have been engaged by the Iranian

Defence Ministry. But the Iranians say they worked for the civilian Atomic Energy Organisation of Iran. The IAEA have reported their satisfaction that the Kimia Maadan company had been created in May 2000 solely for the purpose of designing, procuring and installing ore processing equipment. This work could only be carried through when the nuclear agency furnished it with the technical drawings and reports which formed the basis of the contract.

'Information and explanations provided by Iran were supported by the documentation, the content of which is consistent with the information already available to the Agency', sources in the IAEA summed up. There have been other allegations about fraud in connection with this case, and the Central Intelligence Agency has declined to comment.

Forgeries have been rather popular with the American intelligence services. The forged documents from Niger which 'proved' that Niger was supplying uranium oxide to Iraq were a significant part of the White House's case for the Iraq war. Mohamed ElBaradei wrote to the White House and the National Security Council three months before the Americans launched their war on Iraq, warning them that the Niger documents were likely to be forgeries, and should not be used to stand up allegations about the Iraqi intention to obtain nuclear weapons. It was only when he received no response from the Bush administration that ElBaradei went public to expose the Niger forgeries.

Contentious though the previous allegations on Iraq had been, these allegations about Iran have not come at a propitious time for the outgoing American administration, because there are fairly strong reasons to suspect that the Russian and Chinese representatives on the Security Council may now prove more agnostic about such claims than they had been in previous years.

The chance of renewing the programme of UN sanctions, leave alone extending it, must have receded. Of course, we have no way of accurately predicting the likely responses of the new administration. Will it wish to reopen meaningful talks with the Iranians? Will it willingly pull back from confrontation and diplomatic pressures? Or will it try to defend the dubious practices of the previous administration, and the dubious intelligence upon which they were based? Various ambivalences have been reported concerning the views of the Bush Presidency on these matters. Will peace be made in Iran in order to deploy further afield? Are those forces to be committed to Afghanistan? Or, more likely, as we already warned[1], to Pakistan, an altogether more rational, if dangerous, target. Pakistan has Islamists a-plenty, nuclear weapons, a sufficiency of external

'Obama's first two crucial appointments represent a denial of the wishes of his supporters on the principal issues on which they voted. The vice-president-elect, Joe Biden, is a proud warmaker and Zionist. Rahm Emanuel, who is to be the all-important White House chief of staff, is ... an "Israel-first" Zionist who served in the Israeli army and opposes meaningful justice for the Palestinians.'

John Pilger

enemies, internal schisms and terrorist potential over and above that fostered by the Americans. Pakistan is the sixth most populous nation in the world, the second among Muslim states, and has a prime geostrategic position for would-be world dominators. Perhaps that is why so many of its people nurture suspicions about American goodwill.

The last time that we discussed the likelihood of an Obama presidency, we did warn about one advice stream that will certainly bring influence to bear on the President Elect. This was the eminent foreign policy adviser, Zbig Brzezinski, himself no slouch in the domination stakes. He has now published a debate with Brent Scowcroft,[2] who was also a national security advisor for Presidents George H. W. Bush and Gerald Ford. (Zbig Brzezinski had occupied that position for President Carter.) This debate, moderated by David Ignatius, shows both men in a relaxed mood, and emphasises their urbanity. But Scowcroft is markedly less hawkish than his Democrat interlocutor. Even so, Brzezinski tells us that if the Democrats win the elections, they will certainly slow down the process of installing missile interceptor systems in Poland and the Czech Republic. These systems are supposed to defend the Europeans, who have not asked for them, and they are supposed to render the Czechs, for example, safe from attack by Iranian missiles which don't yet exist, and may never do so.

As Brzezinski rightly tells us:

'I don't see the rush ... the system we want to deploy is non-existent, and the threat against which it is to be deployed is also non-existent.'

We should not forget that one of the reasons advanced by members of the outgoing American administration for hastily including Georgia in Nato was that this would give Nato the reach to enable bombers to strike Iran. What Iran has to do with a *North Atlantic* Treaty is yet to be explained. And what will be the attitude of the Obama presidency to the stand-off in the Caucasus is yet to be clarified. However, it is not very likely that other key Nato allies will hasten to conform to American pressures to enlarge

Nato to include either Georgia or Ukraine, even if the British do hasten to comply with every trans-Atlantic whim.

What will be the outcome of an Obama White House in respect of the present wars? There are high hopes of significant withdrawals of troops from Iraq. We must wait upon events, but, as we have seen, the talk is of redeploying some of the forces engaged in Iraq in Afghanistan, which is regarded as a 'good war' in contrast to the bad one in Iraq.

The BBC reported on the 14th November that:

> 'Up to 2,000 extra British troops are likely to be sent to Afghanistan next year. Ministers are considering sending reinforcements to Afghanistan to meet an expected request from Barack Obama.'

The Ministry of Defence in Britain has stated that no requests have been received from the United States for additional troops, and various British Generals and other officers have made public statements about the undesirability of committing further forces in that theatre. Afghan President Karzai visited Gordon Brown in mid-November however, and did appeal for an increase in the number of soldiers from Britain. Various British Ministers have, more or less tentatively, suggested that any surge in the forces on the ground in Afghanistan should be based upon the principle of 'burden sharing', which would imply that other Nato allies would send additional troops, where necessary changing their rules of engagement to allow them to undertake combat duties.

An Obama surge in Afghanistan does appear to be probable, although it is not known what might be its remit. Meantime, 8,000 British troops are deployed mainly in Helmand Province, where the action is very intense.

The British Secretary for Defence, John Hutton, has declared that these troops are defending very significant British interests, and are crucial to British national security. We are not sure which vital interests are at stake. Would it be vitally interesting to stay in Afghanistan in order to mitigate American belligerence in Pakistan? (Perhaps this might prevent unrest in

---

'All you had to do was look at that array of Clinton-era economic types and CEOs behind Obama at his first news conference to think: been there, done that. The full photo of his economic team that day offered a striking profile of pre-Bush era Washington and the Washington Consensus, and so a hint of the Democratic world the new president will walk into on January 20, 2009.'

Tom Engelhardt

Bradford?) Or, more likely, is it vitally interesting, in the immortal words of a former Ambassador to Washington, 'to get up the arse of the administration and stay there'?

In the absence of more persuasive arguments, the British people have been giving their answer to the claimed vitality of this mission. Sixty-eight per cent of those polled by the BBC, fifty-nine percent of these being men and seventy-five per cent being women, said that British troops should be withdrawn within twelve months. The Afghan Embassy's political affairs secretary said that this was unrealistic. We should not expect a force of 8,000 to 'just abandon the country'. The age group which was most strongly opposed to the war, unsurprisingly, consisted of eighteen to twenty-four year olds, three-quarters of whom said they wanted the troops pulled out. Opposition to the deployment was also very strong among older people.

The columnist Simon Jenkins was asked by the BBC to comment, and he recommended Government to take notice of the survey.

> 'It has never received a popular mandate for this work in any realistic sense. It was done at the bidding of the Americans – there is a new American President, we might be able to capture something from that. But he is equally in favour of it. I just think we should pull out.'

All around the world there remain problems, some of which have been maturing into crises. As Martin Wolf of the *Financial Times* reported

> 'The new President's agenda is daunting. His country's power is also reduced. Indeed, it was never as great as those who spoke of the "unipolar moment" believed. But the US remains the world's greatest power and only leader. It possesses unmatched assets. The presidency of George W. Bush was a lesson in how not to use them. The Obama presidency must now be the opposite.'[3]

With new reversible Clinton guidance?

At the top of Mr. Wolf's agenda, rightly, is economic policy. Many of Obama's election promises, as he so energetically toured the country, involved more or less protectionist policies. But the liberal advisors whose hopes have been raised to the heights in recent days have been concerned, like Mr. Wolf, to maximise the achievements of open global competition. Similar considerations will touch the evolution of policy on the environment.

Nowhere will it be possible to provide one-country solutions to these kinds of problems. Indeed, it is unlikely to be possible to find solutions in one bloc. The Americans have all the debts, the Chinese have all the money, and the Russians have all the energy. If East is East and West is

West and never the twain shall meet, then the future of the capitalist world economy may, in the absence of effective international government, as the prophet Hobbes once told us, be 'nasty, brutish and short'. This judgement seems uncomfortably close in these dismal days. Who knows what other futures may lie in store?

Ken Coates

Footnotes
1. See *Spokesman 99* p12, pp 15-25.
2. Zbigniew Brzezinski and Brent Scowcroft, moderated by David Ignatius: *America and the World: Conversations on the Future of American Foreign Policy,* Basic Books, $25.50.
3. *Financial Times*, 11 November 2008.

COMMUNICATION WORKERS UNION

End the occupation of Iraq and Afghanistan

Billy Hayes
General Secretary

Davie Bowman
President

Meltdown Election

Noam Chomsky

Noam Chomsky is well known to readers of The Spokesman. *A selection of his writings in linguistics and politics has just been published under the title* The Essential Chomsky, *edited by Anthony Arnove (The Bodley Head, £14.99).*

The simultaneous unfolding of the US presidential campaign and unravelling of the financial markets presents one of those occasions where the political and economic systems starkly reveal their nature. Passion about the campaign may not be universally shared, but almost everybody can feel the anxiety from the foreclosure of a million homes, and concerns about jobs, savings and healthcare at risk. The initial Bush proposals to deal with the crisis so reeked of totalitarianism that they were quickly modified. Under intense lobbyist pressure, they were reshaped as 'a clear win for the largest institutions in the system … a way of dumping assets without having to fail or close', as described by James Rickards, who negotiated the federal bailout for the hedge fund Long Term Capital Management in 1998, reminding us that we are treading familiar turf.

The immediate origins of the current meltdown lie in the collapse of the housing bubble supervised by Federal Reserve chairman Alan Greenspan, which sustained the struggling economy through the Bush years by debt-based consumer spending along with borrowing from abroad. But the roots are deeper. In part they lie in the triumph of financial liberalisation in the past 30 years – that is, freeing the markets as much as possible from government regulation. These steps predictably increased the frequency and depth of severe reversals, which now threaten to bring about the worst crisis since the Great Depression.

Also predictably, the narrow sectors that reaped enormous profits from liberalisation are calling for massive state intervention to rescue collapsing financial institutions.

Such interventionism is a regular feature of state capitalism, though the scale today is unusual. A study by international economists Winfried Ruigrok and Rob van Tulder 15 years ago found that at least 20 companies in the Fortune 100 would not have survived if they had not been saved by their respective governments, and that many of the rest gained substantially by demanding that governments 'socialise their losses', as in today's taxpayer-financed bailout. Such government intervention 'has been the rule rather than the exception over the past two centuries', they conclude.

In a functioning democratic society, a political campaign would address such fundamental issues, looking into root causes and cures, and proposing the means by which people suffering the consequences can take effective control.

The financial market 'underprices risk' and is 'systematically inefficient', as economists John Eatwell and Lance Taylor wrote a decade ago, warning of the extreme dangers of financial liberalisation and reviewing the substantial costs already incurred – and proposing solutions, which have been ignored. One factor is failure to calculate the costs to those who do not participate in transactions. These 'externalities' can be huge. Ignoring systemic risk leads to more risk-taking than would take place in an efficient economy, even by the narrowest measures.

The task of financial institutions is to take risks and, if well managed, to ensure that potential losses to themselves will be covered. The emphasis is on 'to themselves'. Under state capitalist rules, it is not their business to consider the cost to others – the 'externalities' of decent survival – if their practices lead to financial crisis, as they regularly do.

Financial liberalisation has effects well beyond the economy. It has long been understood that it is a powerful weapon against democracy. Free capital movement creates what some have called a 'virtual parliament' of investors and lenders, who closely monitor government programmes and 'vote' against them if they are considered irrational: for the benefit of people, rather than concentrated private power. Investors and lenders can 'vote' by capital flight, attacks on currencies, and other devices offered by financial liberalisation. That is one reason why the Bretton Woods system established by the United States and Britain after the Second World War instituted capital controls and regulated currencies.[1]

The Great Depression and the War had aroused powerful radical democratic currents, ranging from the anti-fascist resistance to working class organisation. These pressures made it necessary to permit social democratic policies. The Bretton Woods system was designed in part to create a space for government action responding to public will – for some measure of democracy. John Maynard Keynes, the British negotiator, considered the most important achievement of Bretton Woods to be the establishment of the right of governments to restrict capital movement.

In dramatic contrast, in the neoliberal phase after the breakdown of the Bretton Woods system in the 1970s, the US treasury now regards free capital mobility as a 'fundamental right', unlike such alleged 'rights' as those guaranteed by the Universal Declaration of Human Rights: health, education, decent employment, security and other rights that the Reagan and Bush administrations have dismissed as 'letters to Santa Claus', 'preposterous', mere 'myths'.

In earlier years, the public had not been much of a problem. The reasons are reviewed by Barry Eichengreen in his standard scholarly history of the international monetary system. He explains that in the 19th century, governments had not yet been 'politicised by universal male suffrage and the rise of trade unionism and parliamentary labour parties'. Therefore, the severe costs imposed by the virtual parliament could be transferred to the general population. But with the radicalisation of the general public during the Great Depression and the anti-fascist war, that luxury was no longer available to private power and wealth. Hence in the Bretton Woods system, 'limits on capital mobility substituted for limits on democracy as a source of insulation from market pressures'.

The obvious corollary is that after the dismantling of the post-war system, democracy is restricted. It has therefore become necessary to control and marginalise the public in some fashion, processes particularly evident in the more business-run societies like the United States. The management of electoral extravaganzas by the public relations industry is one illustration. 'Politics is the shadow cast on society by big business,' concluded America's leading 20th century social philosopher John Dewey, and will remain so as long as power resides in 'business for private profit through private control of banking, land, industry, reinforced by command of the press, press agents and other means of publicity and propaganda'.

The United States effectively has a one-party system, the business party, with two factions, Republicans and Democrats. There are differences between them. In his study *Unequal Democracy: The Political Economy of the New Gilded Age*, Larry Bartels shows that during the past six decades 'real incomes of middle-class families have grown twice as fast under Democrats as they have under Republicans, while the real incomes of working-poor families have grown six times as fast under Democrats as they have under Republicans'.

Differences can be detected in this election as well. Voters should consider them, but without illusions about the political parties, and with the recognition that consistently over the centuries, progressive legislation and social welfare have been won by popular struggles, not gifts from above. Those struggles follow a cycle of success and setback. They must be waged every day, not just once every four years, always with the goal of creating a genuinely responsive democratic society, from the voting booth to the workplace.

Footnote

1 The Bretton Woods system of global financial management was created by 730 delegates from all 44 Allied Second World War nations who attended a UN-hosted Monetary and Financial Conference at the Mount Washington Hotel in Bretton Woods in New Hampshire in 1944.

Bretton Woods, which collapsed in 1971, was the system of rules, institutions, and procedures that regulated the international monetary system, under which were set up the International Bank for Reconstruction and Development (IBRD) (now one of five institutions in the World Bank Group) and the International Monetary Fund (IMF), which came into effect in 1945.

The chief feature of Bretton Woods was an obligation for each country to adopt a monetary policy that maintained the exchange rate of its currency within a fixed value.

The system collapsed when the US suspended convertibility from dollars to gold. This created the unique situation whereby the US dollar became the 'reserve currency' for the other countries within Bretton Woods.

With grateful acknowledgements to Noam Chomsky and New York Times Syndicate.

South Ossetia

Epicentre of geopolitical change

*Roy Medvedev
and
Zhores Medvedev*

*During the 1970s,
Spokesman published a
number of books by the
brothers Medvedev,
including notably* Let
History Judge *(1975).
There followed* Political
Essays *and* On Socialist
Democracy, *also by Roy
Medvedev, and* National
Frontiers and International
Scientific Co-operation
and Secrecy of
Correspondence is
Guaranteed by Law, *both
by Zhores Medvedev.*

*Both brothers were among
the first signatories of the
so-called 'Russell Appeal'
which launched the
movement for European
Nuclear Disarmament.*

Some fragments of history

South Ossetia is separated from its principal northern half by spurs from Mount Kazbek that form the Caucasus Mountains. Recent events there have changed the political and economic history of the world, having returned Russia to the status of a 'great power'. This is guaranteed by virtue of Russia's influence, rather than the statistics of consumption.

The ancient Ossetian people's division into 'north' and 'south' has diminished only recently, thanks to the construction, between 1981 and 1985, of the almost four-kilometre long Roki tunnel, built at a height of three kilometres beneath Mount Sokhs. The Ossetians voluntarily became part of the Russian Empire, but in two stages. North Ossetia joined with Russia in 1767. Vladikavkaz, Russia's first fortress in the Northern Caucasus, was built in 1784. South Ossetia became part of Russia in 1801, together with Georgia, which was fragmented at that time into several principalities and kingdoms seeking protection from Russia against raids by the armies of the Persian and Ottoman Empires. The Ossetian people were driven from their historic lands in the southern reaches of the Don Valley by the Mongol invasions, finding refuge in the Caucasus Mountains. The North Ossetians, who were farmers and herdsmen, never experienced serfdom. The South Ossetians became serfs of the Georgian princes Eristavov and Machabeli. Tsar Alexander the Second's Manifest, which abolished serfdom in Russia in 1861, was extended to South Ossetia only in 1864.

The South Ossetian autonomous area

was declared in 1922. In 1991, the autonomous rights of the South Ossetians were revoked by the first president of Georgia, Zviad Gamsakhurdiya, in accordance with his programme of 'Georgia for the Georgians'. The South Ossetian autonomous area was renamed 'Samchabalo', after the family of the Georgian princes of Machabeli. It was forbidden to teach the Ossetian language at school. The uprising of the Ossetians, and then of the Abkhazians, against Gamsakhurdia's decrees led to bloody wars, the defeat of Georgia, and to the appearance of the unrecognised republics of South Ossetia and Abkhazia in 1992 and 1994 respectively. Such a situation could only continue as long as Nato did not expand eastwards, ultimately to include Georgia.

The main strategic opponents of the United States, after the dissolution of the Soviet Union and the end of the 'Cold War', were not far from the trans-Caucasus. They were Iraq, Iran and Afghanistan. The significant increase in the price of oil due to rising demand gave this region greater importance also for the European Union. The independence of the small, unrecognised mini-state of South Ossetia, with a territory of 3,900 square kilometres, became a hindrance to the political and economic programmes of 'the West'.

Nato and Georgia

The end of the 'Cold War' and the disintegration of the Soviet Union could have led to Nato's liquidation since this military bloc had lost its strategic 'opponent'. But, contrary to its own promises and political logic, and under the influence of the United States, Nato adopted a policy of enlargement to the East, recruiting new members from among its former opponents. However, the rapid increase in the number of members of Nato weakened the economic base of this military organisation, particularly because all the Eastern European countries were almost completely dependent on Russia for sources of energy. If the energy balance in France is that 16% of its gas and 12% of its oil comes from Russia, in Italy 29% and 16%, and in Great Britain 2% and 17%, then the position of Eastern Europe with respect to gas and oil is completely different, not to mention Eastern Europe's complete dependence on Russia for nuclear generation of electricity. Estonia, Latvia, Lithuania, Slovakia, Hungary, Bulgaria, Poland and Romania depend on Russia for almost 100% of their gas and between 60 and 100% of their oil. All the nuclear power stations in Eastern Europe and Ukraine were built by the Soviet Union, and require uranium from Russia. Russia guarantees the reprocessing of their spent nuclear fuel. The switching of Nato military operations to the Asiatic region, particularly

Afghanistan and Iraq, has led to the organisation's dependence on Russia and Central Asian countries for air and overland transport communications. In normal circumstances this situation would quickly lead to improving all forms of co-operation between Nato, the European Union and Russia. However, this tendency contradicts the political and military interests of the United States, since it enhances Russia's role in world politics. Closer relations between Russia and the European Union are opposed by Poland, Estonia, Latvia, Lithuania, Hungary and the Czech Republic, where Russophobia forms part of national ideology.

Nato's critical dependence on the energy resources of Russia and Central Asia has led the United States not only to absorb by military means ownership of the native resources of Iraqi oil, but also to plan complete control over the oil and gas reserves of the Caspian region, energy resources which are reckoned to be almost equivalent to those of the Persian Gulf.

'Caspian oil is the best instrument for geo-economically bringing Central Asia and the Trans-Caucasus into world markets, to separate them from Russia, and to liquidate for ever the possibility of post-Soviet imperial integration,' declared Zbigniew Brzezinski, the influential advisor and former strategist of the US State Department, ten years ago. In order to realise this plan, in 1996, an oil pipeline from Baku to Tbilisi to Ceyhan (BTC) was proposed, which was especially important for Georgia, struggling with economic decline. It would have been much easier and cheaper to send Baku oil to coastal terminals via Armenia and Iran. However, Armenia's participation was opposed by Azerbaijan, and the United States opposed Iran's. The chosen route, 449 kilometres in Azerbaijan, 235km in Georgia, and 1,059km in Turkey, was dearer and technically more complex, and passed through Kurdish regions of Turkey, so that it took a long time to find sponsors. In the end, construction of the pipeline began in 2003, paid for by 11 oil companies, including British Petroleum and the Azerbaijan Oil Company as the main backers.

The problem of supplying natural gas to the European Union outside Russian territory was partly resolved by the 'Baku-Tbilisi-Erzurum' pipeline, which commenced operations at the end of 2006. It undoubtedly reduced Georgia's dependence on Russian gas. However, the real reserves of oil and gas in Azerbaijan turned out to be significantly more modest than expected. The resources of this region, which has supplied Russia, the Soviet Union and Europe with oil and gas for almost 150 years, are badly exhausted. The Baku-Tbilisi-Ceyhan pipeline has for a while not operated at its projected capacity, nor is it profitable. In order to guarantee Europe's oil and gas supplies in the long term by going around Russia, it is necessary to look to the southern route for the oil and gas resources of Kazakhstan, Uzbekistan and Turkmenistan. Since the end of 2006, Kazakhstan began to send oil by tanker across the Caspian Sea from Aktau to Baku for onward transportation via the Baku-Tbilisi-Ceyhan pipeline. Part of the Baku and Kazakh oil was sent by pipeline to the Georgian port of Supse, where it is transferred to tankers, and the terminal can handle about five million tonnes of oil a year. The Nabucco project has been put forward in an attempt to solve the 'gas' problems of Eastern Europe, with not only Georgia but also Ukraine participating. It was precisely these projects of transporting energy resources through Georgia to the European Union, and circumventing Russia, that made Georgia's membership of Nato so important.

Georgia and the Nabucco Pipeline

Project 'Nabucco', named in honour of Verdi's opera first performed in Milan in 1848, arose somewhat later. But it was not so much Verdi's music that played a part in the choice of name as the subject of the opera, concerning events in Babylon, one of the most notable cities of antiquity, the ruins of which attracted many explorers to Iraq. The Nabucco pipeline might run not far from these ruins. The route of the pipeline is planned to go from Azerbaijan and Georgia into Turkey, then further into Bulgaria, Romania, Hungary, the Czech Republic and Austria. But there is not enough Azerbaijan gas to fill the pipeline, and only the somewhat richer gas resources of Turkmenistan and Kazakhstan can guarantee to meet the demands of Eastern Europe. Gas pipelines, as distinct from oil ones, can run along the seabed. However, the countries of Eastern Europe, not having had serious conflicts with Iran, were ready to build a gas pipeline on Iranian territory, using Iranian gas. Iran has the second largest natural gas reserves in the world after Russia. Georgia's membership of Nato was considered as a guarantee of all these oil and gas pipeline systems.

Arming Georgia

The establishment in Georgia of efficient military units and their armaments was actively begun in 2004, mainly for a forced solution of the South Ossetia and Abkhazia problems. There was simply no other reason for the rapid militarisation of this small country which had no military tradition. This, of course, was understood in Abkhazia, South Ossetia, and in Russia. The territorial conflicts, which had been going on in Georgia since 1992, prevented the country's acceptance into Nato. They could either have left these territories a free choice, rather like Cyprus, or returned their promised broad autonomy. However, antagonisms between former members of the Georgian Federation go back too far. That left only the military variant, which was approved not only by the United States, but also by several Nato member countries, and also by Israel and Ukraine, which had begun to supply large amounts of modern armaments to Georgia, including anti-aircraft systems, instructors, and even military uniforms. Georgian soldiers were also trained in the role of Special Forces, which they practised in Iraq, where the Georgian contingent was rotated. Georgian and American units undertook joint manoeuvres. But all these measures were not enough to establish military efficiency for the entire nation. This quality can be instilled only by history and by state experience, which form the psychology of a people. Georgians simply did not know what real war was. Georgia was never a colony of Russia, she was a privileged protectorate.

The main errors in this plan were the dates. In 2004, nobody expected that wars in Iraq and Afghanistan would continue without any apparent victory for four more years, broadening in their scale. If these wars had been finished sooner, freeing the American Army, Navy and Air Force, together with Georgia joining Nato, then the blitzkrieg in South Ossetia and Abkhazia might have had some hope of success. American military bases would have been established on Georgian territory, not only for the protection of that country, but also for the possibility of war with Iran. In winter all the passes, tunnels and roads through the Caucasus mountains are completely closed by snow and impassable to military equipment. Pentagon experts always judge the capability of the Russian Army by the results of the Chechen campaign. It was thought that Dmitry Medvedev, as a new commander in chief, would display indecisiveness and reluctance to take risks.

Results and consequences of events in Georgia

Oil and sea pipelines passing through Georgia's territory were, naturally, inactive for two to three weeks while military activity continued. The transportation of oil by barge and tanker from Kazakhstan was also stopped. Azerbaijan sent its oil through the Russian pipeline to the terminal in Novorossisk. The Nabucco gas pipeline project, on which construction has not yet begun, has become more difficult to realise. According to the headline of one of the commentaries on US Vice President Dick Cheney's visit to Baku, Tbilisi and Kiev at the beginning of September 2008, 'Cheney flies to the Caucasus to save Nabucco, but sentence on the project has already been handed down'. The main potential sources of gas for this pipeline, Kazakhstan and Turkmenistan, have already decided to send their deliveries to China and Russia. For them the main problem was the price of gas, particularly the very low price paid by Ukraine. China and Russia proposed market prices and reliable transit. To find sufficient capital to build Nabucco, which is more than 3,300km long, at a cost approaching six billion dollars, is now practically unrealistic.

The construction of American bases in Georgia has been deferred for an indefinite period. The arrival of the American naval fleet off the coast of Georgia, preposterously to deliver 'humanitarian aid', followed by the appearance of Nato warships and various announcements by President Yushchenko who tried, without effect, to limit the movements of the Russian Black Sea fleet, have given rise to political complications in the Ukraine. Now it has become clear that Russia's Black Sea fleet will remain in Sevastopol for the foreseeable future, preventing any real possibility of Nato membership for Ukraine. The full history of President Saakashvili's fateful instruction to commence the massive bombardment of South Ossetia, delivered by mobile phone from Tbilisi at midnight on 7 August 2008, timed to coincide with the beginning of the Olympic games in Beijing, remains unclear. A study of all the 'Georgian' details of this short war is possible only in Tbilisi, where both authors of this article were born in 1925.

Translated by Tony Simpson

RMT

Fighting for Trade Union freedom

Build peace not bombs

Bob Crow
General Secretary

John Leach
President

From A To X

John Berger

From A to X *is a novel in
letters, a correspondence
between A'ida and her
lover, Xavier, who has
been put in prison as a
member of the resistance.
But this is a one-sided
correspondence, because
we only have A'ida's
touching letters, and
Xavier's brief notes on the
back of some of them.
These were recovered from
some rudimentary files left
in the old prison from
which Xavier has recently
been relocated to a new
high security unit outside
the town.*

Mi Golondrino,

Two winters ago I think it was, I
mentioned a man to you, a diabetic who
came one night to the pharmacy in urgent
need of sugar. Did I tell you? He was beside
himself, but as chance would have it, I
happened to be there. I gave him what he
needed and he left. He spoke with an accent
and I didn't ask him where he was from and
he didn't give me his name. Because I talk
to you so often in my head, I sometimes get
muddled about what I've put or haven't put
into my letters. In a city without prisons –
has there ever been one? – who would ever
guess one can put so much into letters?

I reread your letters many times. Not at
night. Rereading them then tends to be
dangerous for the night. I read them in the
morning after coffee and before work. I go
outside so I can see the sky and the
horizons. Often I go up onto the roof. At
other times I go outside, cross the road and
sit on the fallen tree, where the ants are.
Yes, still. I take your letter out of its soiled
envelope and I read. And as I read the days
between clatter past like the freight wagons
of a train! And what do I mean by the days
between? Between this time and the last
time I read the same letter. And between the
day you wrote it and the day they took you.
And between the day one of the herders
posted it and the day I'm sitting on the roof
reading it. And between this day when we
have to remember everything and the day
when we'll be able to forget because we
have all. These, my love, are the days
between, and the closest railway to here is
two hundred kilometres away.

This morning I was in your Suse buying
a new pack of cards. I was crossing the

market where the orange stalls are, and a man steps from behind me and says:

I owe you a word of thanks.

Thanks? Why?

Two years ago in Sucrat you saved my life.

How come?

A shot of sugar.

You mean sugar or an amphetamine?

Late one night.

It was then I remembered him and his weighed-down shoulders and his curious accent and his anger, his anger that had signalled how low his sugar-count probably was. He was the man I think I told you about who came that night to the pharmacy.

I'm living in the next street, behind the barber's, he says, please be my guest so I can offer you a coffee. It's two years I've been waiting.

I don't have much time.

I work as a cleaner in the market and I have to begin in an hour, so a quick coffee.

If you wish.

We went down a narrow passageway beside the barber's.

There, he says, nodding to the men having their hair cut and being shaved – more truths come out there than in most prayers!

You've been working in the market for long?

Five years, ever since I took the decision to follow my vocation.

Vocation?

By way of reply, he unlocks a front door, which opens outward and extends his arm in a gesture of invitation for me to enter.

It's bare, but I beg you make yourself at home. Italian coffee or Turkish?

Whichever is easiest

It's simply a question of how I grind it.

He disappeared into a kind of closet which gave on to a corner of the room, and plugged in a coffee grinder. An aroma of coffee as astringent as resin, filled the room.

The room was small It must have been a small shop. Perhaps a haberdasher's. There was a tight, neat roll of bedding on the floor against one wall, a large table before a window, and two stools. Nothing else. No curtains, no rugs, no pictures, no overhead lighting. A reading lamp on the table.

Your coffee smells good.

You can judge, my honourable guest, when you've tasted it.

May I ask about your vocation?

My vocation, he replied standing in the doorway of the closet, was to be a poet.

Was?

It was settled long before I knew it. It took me thirty years to figure it out. Before that I sold carpets. It's still my vocation, needless to say, if you wish you can look on my table.

On the long table in front of the window, a dozen sheets of paper, the same size, and carefully aligned – like stepping stones – were laid out from left to right. Each one was covered with a small neat handwriting, frequently corrected or crossed-out. Beside certain passages a large question mark had been pencilled in; occasionally beside a passage there was a tick.

The regular left margin of each page and the differing lengths of the short lines showed it was being written as poetry. Several other sheets covered with the same close writing waited on the windowsill. I couldn't read a single word. It looked like Turkish. I asked him.

Yes and no. I write in the language of the Taurus mountains, this is my mother tongue. She's alone all day and wants to hear stories in the evening.

He gave me a special look as if he was checking to make sure that I recognised how things were not as they seemed to be. Certain beggars do the same after being given alms: their look says – thank me for having chosen you!

I went over to see what he was doing in the closet. The coffee in the copper pot had risen twice and he was adding the last spoonful of cold water. Wherever there was a space on a horizontal surface in the closet – near the gas-ring, beside the basin, under the mirror – there were single sheets of paper covered with the same meticulous handwriting. He watched me noticing this.

I move around when I'm working, particularly in the early morning before the sun's up. If it doesn't come to me by the big table, I take a stool and sit by the front door or I wander out here to eat some bread or brush my teeth.

I move around from valley to valley, from Mount Ararat to the Heights of Goksul or to the Passes of Cilicie.

Again he gave me the beggar look.

Then he handed me my cup of coffee. I sipped. It was the best I'd tasted for a long while. I installed myself on one of the stools near the table.

Is it one long poem?

Maybe no poet writes more than one and it takes a lifetime. He thinks he's writing different short poems but really they're all part of the same long one.

What's it about?

It's in praise of life and its abundance. When I'm sweeping in the market, I listen, I never stop listening and often the words I hear are so well chosen, I remember them. A question of keeping your ears open — diabetics, as you must know, run a higher risk than most of becoming both deaf and blind.

You could translate a line or two for me? I ask.

The coffee pleases you?

It's remarkable.

You can still taste it between your eyes forty minutes after you've drunk it — provided everything else is calm. Yesterday we had a rocket from one of their Apaches.

A few lines?

I wanted to offer you a coffee and show you my secret because I think you saved my life.

A few lines?

I'll read you some lines then without translating. You'll hear the secret and it'll still be a secret.

The sound of his voice in the room changed, and it was as if we were sitting under a tree. I let the words pass without asking anything of them. Then he said:

We tend to think secrets are small, no? like precious jewels or sharp stones or knives that can be hidden and kept secret because they're small. But there are also secrets which are huge, and it is because of their immensity that they remain hidden except to those who have tried to put their arms around them. These secrets are promises.

He gave me another beggar look

I drank the last dregs of the delicious coffee, I thanked him, and as I was leaving, he pronounced his name for the first time: Hasan.

Writing this to you late tonight I think of your letters which I reread early in the mornings when the days between clatter past like freight wagons, and I think of my letters that you read in your cell, and I smile at their immense secret which is ours, yours and mine.

We are very grateful for permission to reprint a chapter of From A to X, A Story in Letters *by John Berger (Verso, 2008).*

Weapons for Pensions

How social security became national security

Richard Minns

Richard Minns is an independent researcher based in Buenos Aires and London. He is the author of The Cold War in Welfare: Stock Markets versus Pensions *(Verso).*

A Dedication

To the people of Argentina whose pensions helped pay for the so-called 'odious' debt[1] used to buy British, French and US helicopters, which were then used to throw their tortured children and friends into the Atlantic and Pacific – the 30,000 'disappeared' in Argentina, 9,000 in Chile, and countless others in neighbouring countries. This especially includes Jewish citizens under Argentinian and Chilean governments, which welcomed ex-Nazis planning the Third World War – against communism (Goni, 2003; Mount, 2002). Jewish deaths were over-represented in the final toll of 'the disappeared', while Israel supplied weapons (Rein, 2003). The US Secretary of State, Henry Kissinger, condoned these crimes against humanity in the battle against alleged communism and dissidence (*The Guardian*, December 12, 2003, 'Kissinger Approved Argentinian Dirty War') and helped to supply the weapons by various means. The UK Labour governments, under Harold Wilson and James Callaghan, prior to that Conservative Edward Heath, and latterly Margaret Thatcher, and the labour movement were variously preoccupied with three-day weeks, public sector strikes and confrontation with trade unions. Like Israel and its supply of weapons which killed Jews, the weapons flowed to dictatorships where trade unionists were being killed.

The US Central Intelligence Agency orchestrated a coup in Chile which brought Augusto Pinochet to power, and killed (euphemistically called suicide) democratically-elected Salvador Allende (latest allegation to emerge is that Allende was a Soviet spy) on the original 9/11 (1973). It funded 'Operation Condor' to pursue and murder dissidents fleeing from one South American country to another – Argentina, Chile, Brazil, Uruguay, Bolivia, Paraguay (Calloni,1999). The final cost of the US, UK, French, Austrian, German, Italian and Israeli helicopters, jet fighters, anti-tank guns, frigates, surface-to-air-missiles, armoured cars and small arms fell on all pensioners, tens of thousands of whom in Argentina and Chile had already lost their children, without trace.

Latin American countries were then introduced by the US-controlled World Bank to private pensions, which allegedly offered a solution to the enormous debt incurred by weapons purchases (debt figures and arms purchases follow below). The case was not presented like this of course, rather one of restoring economic prosperity and social security through the enhancement of financial markets. Chile was the exemplar of private pensions 'reform' where the 'burden' of state pensions was to be eliminated, paraded by the World Bank to other countries in South America and to post-Communist Eastern Europe, whose representatives were flown to Chile to learn from the post-coup experiment. The main Chilean adviser also discussed the privatisation of pensions with Margaret Thatcher.

Culprits for the indiscriminate treatment of people and their deaths are to this day being identified and sentenced. There are 'wanted' posters in the Argentinian press for some of the criminals with a reward of £20,000. The private pensions solution for the cost of it all is also under serious investigation, in Chile and Argentina in particular. Argentina has re-introduced a revamped state pension option to be raised twice a year against an index of prices and wages. In 2008, as part of the response to the world financial crisis, the President of Argentina proposed to nationalise the private pension system. Her opposite number, the President of Chile, in 2006 had condemned her World Bank-inspired private exemplar, based on an official (Marcel Commission) report.

The system has low coverage, low density of contributions, it leaves almost ninety-five per cent of the independent workers outside the system, it shows very little competition and high commission charges, it does not take into account the complexities of the modern workplace ... and discriminates against women ... amongst other shortcomings (quoted in Kay and Sinha, p. 7).

The Grandmothers of May Square in Argentina, led by Estela de Carlotto, have now discovered 95 of their grandchildren who were given to childless military couples while their parents were killed. The Mothers of May Square, led by Hebe de Bonafini, began the struggle in 1977 (Minns,

2006). They are now all pensioners. The US knew exactly what was occurring, despite its dissembling political commentaries about national defence against communism. The Mothers and Grandmothers of May Square lost their children, *and* also their pensions in order to pay for it all.[2]

That's the story. The point is this. The United States, Israel and Europe (France in particular) continued their relentless weapons supplies, knowing exactly what was going on. The social security budget, I contend, paid for it. My story and interpretation of the reasons for all this slaughter, followed by pension reform to pay the massive 'odious' debt for the weapons which killed 30,000 to 50,000 people, is rather different from the conventional explanation about the rationale and functioning of social welfare, and the alleged need for pension reform and the private provision of pensions.

Questions

Two questions to begin: what are pensions really about? And what have weapons got to do with it? The simple answer is that they both deal with death, natural or premeditated. But the next question is are there connections between them or are they separate matters, both dealing with death, but distinct subjects that we should never, intellectually and politically, connect?

I believe that it is a matter of establishing a framework which, firstly, does not accept conventional explanations for pension reform, and secondly exposes the real reasons for reform. Taking this point by point, I contend that there is a 'cold war in welfare' which pits one model of social security provision for *old* age against another – state versus private, or 'European' and 'Asian-Pacific' versus 'Anglo-American' – while at the same time maintaining a defence industry or military expenditure to provide protection for people of *all* ages, regardless of which part of the model a country belongs to.

This appears complex, but it isn't. I argue that the history of the cold war in welfare and pensions was concerned with cutting, freezing and privatising state systems because the old must contribute their share to 'national security and well-being'. They are now so substantial, accused of being a growing 'burden', a 'doomsday scenario', 'a shock', a potential for state bankruptcy by many commentators such as the World Bank, the London *Financial Times* and others, that their sacrifice will have to equal or outweigh others, in the 'national interest'.

Let us ask ourselves why is it really *so* important to 'reform' pensions? I hope to show that the disputes about welfare and pensions persist as an essential part of a geographical and ideological conflict in which weapons production is still crucial, privatisation of welfare is deemed necessary, and, when push comes to shove, pensions are now used to pay for our broader, life-time defence against adversaries. It's like a pooling of risk; the old are old, but we are all under threat of death *at any age* from external forces, the ubiquitous 'enemies'. There are plenty of enemies around to justify national security. Pensioners should accept their part in societal protection and economic growth, and pay for it since they represent such a potential cost. They may be a vulnerable group. But so are the rest of us.

Pensions are bound up with definitions of social and national security, as well as the arms trade and the defence 'industry'. If we are now all supposed to be more secure after the demise of the communist threat, able to live our lives and retirement without fear of communist invasion and gulags, waiting for the peace dividend to benefit us all, why has expenditure on arms increased and social security/pensions been cut and /or privatised? Why are pensioners, especially women in the UK (1.6 million) and South America (50% of all women will receive no pension despite all the reforms – Gonzales, 2004-5), still figuring so large in poverty figures? At the same time, the UK Labour government (2008), almost without a murmur, is able to commission £4 billion of aircraft carriers, to be followed by £12 billion of US fighter jets to maintain Britain's 'international presence'.

But even that is not what it is really all about. It's about a new definition of the nation state. It is not a 'welfare state'. Instead, it is a 'national security state' (Menjivar and Rodriguez, 2005). I suggest it always has been.

The threat of old age

Social security, in its generous interpretation, recognises vulnerable groups, defined by employment, health, gender or age. The interesting part of the post-Cold War scenario is that old people (and other groups too) are now seen as a major *threat*, their numbers creating a 'shock', rather than a celebration or a concern for generous provision which one might deduce from welfare state ideology. The welfare state helped to protect and insure people's lives. Now there are too many claimants, and 'enemies', to contend with.

This is a belief system, hypothesis, a theory propagated by institutions and commentators from the *Financial Times* to *New Left Review*. From the *Financial Times* the citations about doomsday scenarios are too numerous to mention. I refer to a few in *The Cold War in Welfare* (Minns, 2001). The *New Left Review/Verso* relies on Robin Blackburn's lengthy articles and books where he repeats his obsession with a Meidner plan to rescue us all from the old age 'shock' (his word), and from our financial systems which provide another, rather unsurprising, 'shock' (Blackburn, 2006).

'Shock' seems to be the explanation for whatever you want. Invent a 'shock' and reasoned argument is cast aside. It is the current basis of our political systems, which is to create fear. The 'left' contributes to this scenario. It is not really a shock, despite what the pundits from right and left say, but part of the logic of our financial systems (Klein, 2007, Kindleburger, 1996).

Of course, there is no automatic read-off in my story. Weapons production and defence expenditure do not feature in a zero-sum game where subtraction and addition of financial claims and contributions add up to zero, and in which provision for the old stagnates in real terms or declines proportionately in relation to defence expenditure. Life and politics are not so simple. My contention is that there is compelling evidence that it *can*. Commenting on the recession in Israel in 2002, for example, *Globes* suggested that the reason it was not worse was that the Israeli government increased military spending by 10.7% 'partially financed by cuts in social services' (Klein, 2007, p. 435).

The reasons for social security cuts and privatisation, and the reasons for social security itself, are not what they seem when we consider the arguments about 'national' versus 'social' security. Pensions are not about 'pensions', and never have been. They are just one, subsidiary part of the national security state. Let us continue with some of the evidence and history and try to draw some conclusions.

The need for security: the creation of 'fear'

Britain, preceded by Germany facing the burgeoning SPD (Socialdemokratische Partei Deutschlands), started to improve social conditions at the beginning of the twentieth century. The Russian revolutions of 1905 and 1917 also concentrated the mind. The imperative was 'national efficiency' (Gilbert, 1966) and then 'national reconstruction' ('reconstruction or revolution', Gilbert, 1970). Argentina and Uruguay were also amongst the first to introduce what became known as welfare states. By mid century they had nearly universal state pension systems, along with Brazil, Chile and Costa Rica. Some had admired the corporatist approaches of de Rivera in Spain and Mussolini in Italy (Paul and Paul, 1995).

The original rationale and ideology/pretence of dispassionate and caring welfare now does not exist, if in reality it ever did. The 'cold war in welfare' took over, in which the welfare state myth had to be obliterated. What is now perceived to be a 'threat' of the old, a proverbial 'shock', provided part of the justification for shifting priorities, and ending the myth of the altruistic state. The World Bank believes that, since pensioners rely on future economic growth, they should contribute to it.

> The design of a pension system must explicitly recognise that pension benefits are claims against future economic output. To fulfill [US spelling] their primary goals, pension systems must contribute to future economic output …This requires the inclusion of secondary developmental goals, which seek to create positive developmental outcomes by minimizing the potential negative impacts that pension systems may have on labor and macroeconomic stability while leveraging positive impacts through increased national saving and financial market development. (Holtzman in Kay and Sinha, 2008, p. 178).

In prosaic English this means that pensions as welfare are finished. They must contribute to the national economy and cease their 'distortions' (*translation*, 'cost'). In other words, they must be cut.

Defence and weapons are a different matter. On 10 March 2008, a BBC report stated that the cost of UK military operations in Afghanistan and Iraq was set to almost double to over £3 billion, a 94% increase on the previous year. Bob Ainsworth, Labour's Armed Forces Minister, stated:

> 'The threat changes … We have to stay ahead of the enemy as much as we can and that's not cheap'.

Yet again, an 'enemy'.

Firstly, as Ainsworth inadvertently implies, supporting and subsidising the arms industry is not cheap (certainly not with the extent of bribery which is endemic), but, as an aside, neither is the privatisation of pensions, which involves subsidies and tax concessions – public income foregone (ie. public expenditure) to help the 'market'. The cost of this World Bank favourite varies, but in the UK amounts to £18.9 billion for the year to September 2008. Little if anything is said about the *cost* of private pensions' contribution to economic output. The issue is ulimately about economic interests which 'enemies', 'threats' and 'shocks' help to justify.

Consider the following. The international cartel which supports this equation of private national and social security includes the five permanent members of the UN Security Council who are responsible for 87% of the world's 35$ billion of global arms exports (2007). Two of them are responsible for 80% of global private pension assets (2005). They represent the largest arms manufacturers in the world (the US Lockheed Martin is the largest and the reason for the *Foreign Corrupt Practises Act, 1977* following major bribery allegations about, amongst others, a deal with South Korea);

the largest banks (US Citibank, the largest which piled on the debt to South America to buy weapons), and the largest pension fund managers.

Opposing models in the welfare cold war

I have discussed in more detail the opposing claims in the cold war in welfare (Minns, 2001). The attached Table is a very useful addition showing the binary nature of welfare reform which features in the new cold war (Table 1).

The table tries to show the basic parameters of welfare reform which we can now see as part of the new cold war. The World Bank has been the continuing purveyor of a particular anti-state doctrine of welfare, resting on individual responsibility, savings and capital markets. Its theory maintained that policies for economic growth, savings, and capital markets were consistent with pensions and welfare privatisation – a particular economic development theory, or modernisation theory.

As it unsurprisingly turns out, the promotion of capital markets is not

Table 1 The Cold War of Pension Reform		
	Traditional Logic (1950s-1980s) old Cold War	*Current Logic (1990s-to date), new cold war*
Model for policies and reforms	European countries	Chile
Main types of reform	Unification and system changes in public provision	Privatisation of the public system
Main stimulus	Inequities and inefficiency	Rising pension spending and capital shortage
Main goals	Social	Economic
Main domestic agencies promoting the reforms	Social security institutes; Ministries of Labour	Ministry of Finance, Economy; central banks
Typical background of reform promoters	Lawyers (social security specialists)	Economists (generalists)
Main international agency in the reforms	ILO (International Labour Office)	World Bank

Based on Madrid (2003) Retiring the State, p. 40.

synonymous with economic development and welfare. The World Bank theory produced neither because it depended on financial markets, a questionable contributor to development and welfare as, in passing, we have seen in 2008. As I write (2008), the financial markets and banks are in yet another collapse. But the World Bank aimed to base its theory of welfare and development on this precarious structure for what must be termed ideological reasons.

The explosive political situation in Latin America was an essential part of the development of the privatisation of pensions – a testing-ground for the privatisation experiment which was paraded by the World Bank as the way forward for pensions security and economic growth. The political background involved the support for dictatorships in order to implement reform, the murder of upwards of 50,000 people with weapons and support (financial, advisory, political, security) supplied by the 'West' (USA, UK, France, Israel in particular), and the privatisation of pensions – an article of faith for the World Bank and IMF, although they had their disagreements about its applicability from time to time.

The US façade continues

The weapons and therefore the debt continued despite one of the members of the UN Security Council attempting to control the supply of arms to Argentina. I will paraphrase part of the transcript of the US House Foreign Affairs Committee during its consideration of lifting the embargo on weapons to Argentina after President Carter had gone and Ronald Reagan took over. The paraphrase is based on a *New York Times* report of May 8, 1981.

> *'Military Aid for Argentina Passes Hurdle in House'. The House Foreign Affairs Committee approves a bill ending the three-year ban on military aid to Argentina ... A vote of 20 to 15 turned down an amendment that would have tied aid to tracing 5000 (sic) 'disappeared' since 1978. ... Committee members accused the Argentinian government of condoning the burning of synagogues and other anti-semitic acts. The State Department said that Argentina had done a lot to curb human rights abuses. The 'disappeared' had declined from 1000 in 1975 when the ban was imposed to zero this year ... The State Department representative noted that since the ban Argentina had bought $2 billion in weapons mainly from Europe and Israel. It was stated by the Director of the Defense Security Assistance Agency, before a Senate Foreign Relations Committee, that 'we are sending a signal that the US is committed to cooperating in the collective defense of the hemisphere' (sic).*

The flow of arms from the US resumed, if ever it had really ceased[3] ($1 billion for starters – anti-submarine weapons, 'reconnaissance' aircraft, and equipment for upgrading the Navy), helpfully for Argentina less than one year before it went to war with Britain over the Falklands/Malvinas Islands. US, French, Dutch and Israeli weapons were employed against the British; French 'Roland' missiles were used in the defence of Stanley airport and shot down a British 'Sea Harrier' jet. French 'Exocet' missiles sank two British ships, fired from French Dassault 'Super Etendard' fighter jets. The Argentine cruiser, *The General Belgrano*, which was sunk by *HMS Conqueror,* was originally built in the USA before the Second World War, survived Pearl Harbor, was then sold to Argentina, refitted with UK Parsons turbines, Babcock and Wilson boilers, two British 'Seacat' anti-missile launchers, Dutch search radar, and French 'Alouette' helicopters. The only parts of it which were Argentinian, presumably, were the hundreds of sailors who died in the controversial incident, and the Argentinian flag. The British newspaper, the jingoistic *Sun*, infamously headlined a front-page piece about the sinking, '*Gotcha'*.

The arms trade with South America, in 'defence of the hemisphere' (a perverse geographical abstraction), is maybe one version of history. The cynical profiteering from death, wherever and however, and sacrificing social security/pensions to pay for it, is another. The reality is not about right and wrong, moral or national values, sovereignty or anything else one cares to dream up. It is simply about the business of *death*.

After considering the arms imports and the debt incurred, we shall examine the pensions reforms, noting in passing that, while pensions were privatised , those of the military and other supposedly 'essential' workers – public employees and oil workers – were not (Table 2). One may ask, if privatisation was such a good thing, why were these categories exempt from the social security 'improvements'? The World Bank has never commented on this application of its policies. It may be because the role of the military was paramount; the real purpose of privatisation was buried under a theory of private savings and economic growth which failed. It was really about payment of debt for military expenditure. The military itself was exempt from such payments.

The weapons build-up

Table 3 shows military expenditure as a percentage of GDP for some Latin American countries for 1976 as the weapons build-up was progressing. From 1976 to 1985, Brazil was consistently the lowest in all years except for this one, when it was pipped by Colombia, which subsequently rose to 2-3 times that of Brazil. Many of these countries *except Brazil* subsequently privatised their pension system. Paraguay did not because it

Table 2
Pension Privatisation In Latin America
Dates, Systems, and Opt-outs; (selected countries)

	Argentina	Bolivia	Colombia	Chile	Mexico	Peru	Uruguay
Date Enacted	Sept 93	Nov 96	Dec 93	Nov 80	Dec 95	Dec 92	Sept 95
Date Implemented	July 94	May 97	Apr 94	May 81	July 97	Jun 93	Apr 96
Type of reform	Mixed private/public with options	Private (replacement of the state)	Parallel (Private and public alongside)	Private (replacement)	Private (replacement)	Parallel	Mixed
Groups exempt	Armed forces, provincial and municipal employees	None, but armed forces under special rules	Armed forces, Congress, teachers, oil workers, provincial/municipal employees	Armed forces	Armed forces, most public sector employees, oil workers	Armed forces	Armed forces, bank employees
Management	Domestic and foreign firms, public entities, coops, labour unions	Domestic and foreign firms	Domestic and foreign firms, public and coops	Domestic and foreign firms, labour unions	Domestic and foreign firms, public bodies	Domestic and foreign firms	Domestic and foreign firms public bodies

Based on Madrid (2003) *Retiring the State*, pp 18-20.

Table 3
Military Expenditure as Per Cent of GDP (1976)

Argentina	2.4
Bolivia	3.8
Brazil	1.3
Chile	6.1
Colombia	1.2
Ecuador	2.2
Guyana	8.8
Paraguay	1.7
Peru	5.0
Uruguay	2.2
Venezuela	2.2

Stockholm International Peace Research Institute (SIPRI), *Yearbook, 1977.*

had no state pension system to speak of, perhaps underlining the argument about the use of pensions to pay weapons debt.

Brazil has for years been a major weapons producer, amongst the top ten to twelve in the world (Table 4 for recent figures). In the years 2002-2006, Brazil's weapons exports amounted to ten times those of all other Latin American suppliers put together. This situation has helped historically, I suggest, in Brazil's resistance to pension reform, based on the burden of my argument about weapons-induced debt.

This does not mean a country does not privatise if it is a major weapons producer. Look at the UK as number one producer, US at number two, with

Table 4
Imports and Exports of Weapons 2002-2006
Selected South American Countries

	$millions	
	Imports	*Exports*
Argentina	247	–
Brazil	826	144
Chile	1882	2
Venezuela	596	7

Source; *SIPRI Yearbook, 2007*

the largest private pension systems in the world. It's a matter of balance of payments and local political factors (in the UK the pension system has been predicated on private provision even since the 'path-breaking' Beveridge Report of 1946, much to the chagrin of defenders of the welfare state). It also does not mean that a weapons producer does not have significant debt. But it is not all dead-end unproductive debt, which the purchase of military hardware entails. Nevertheless, Brazil *is* included in tables of 'odious' debt.

The equation is not simple. To boil things down, what we have always left out of the equation is the role of weapons debt. Weapons debt was created and ordinary citizens, especially pensioners in various countries, helped pay for it through the mythology of pension 'reform'. Trade unions in Argentina eventually called it a swindle (Minns, 2007). The increase in Argentinian *military* expenditure is staggering in comparison to other countries, such as Brazil, Chile and Peru (Table 5 on Argentinian military expenditure): hence my emphasis on this country.

Table 5
Argentina: military expenditure, 1970-80, in local currency

Year	1970	1971	1972	1973	1974	1975	1976	1977	1978	1979	1980
Pesos	1799	2171	3424	4434	6387	10308	180379	415518	1187366	3479094	5623165

Source; *Boletin Oficial.* US Library of Congress. Nicole Ball. SIPRI *Yearbook,* 1983, p. 185

Shock in Argentina

President Menem incurred further debt, hooked the currency to the dollar, sold off major companies, further cut public pensions (1994), and introduced a partial privatisation arrangement, leading to what some have described as the reason for the Argentinian financial crisis in 2001. State pensions were still due for payment while contributors opted out – a classic reform disaster of destroying revenue in the face of growing liabilities – of which the World Bank seemed to have no cognizance whatsoever. Historic debt mounted inexorably. Pensions were decimated to pay for all this.

It began with the social security budget in Argentina, run by a key adviser and Rasputin-type figure, Minister of Social Security Jose Lopez Rega (believer in the occult). The budget was plundered to pay for the Triple A death squad (Alianza Anti-Comunista Argentina) in their ubiquitous unmarked Ford Falcons, snatching people off the street. Crimes for which Isabel Peron, President at the time (1974-76), was in 2007 issued with an extradition warrant while she resided in Spain. She was herself arrested and interned by the Videla junta of 1976, supposedly for not being sufficiently ruthless in the face of rising social dissent. She, as ex-head of state, incredibly denies all knowledge of the 2,000 murders which occurred during her presidency, conducted by assassins paid by her Ministry of Social Security.

The World Bank (a public body dependent on international borrowing with a publicly underwritten, generous pension scheme) pontificated about irresponsible, debt-laden republics which needed to rely much more on the market as arbiter of economic development and welfare. With Isabel Peron under house arrest, weapons and debt piling up, Peron herself responsible for 2,000 deaths of her own citizens, and Henry Kissinger, in 1976, giving his approval to the 'dirty war', the World Bank, in its extensive publications about pension reform years later, made no comment about the reasons for the burgeoning debt, the weapons purchases, which were still continuing as the accumulated debt and interest mounted.

Argentina and Menem was the World Bank's opportunity, after Chile, to play around with their theory. They helped to create mayhem, which led to more deaths in 2001, as Argentina unpegged itself from IMF policies, witnessed savings disappear, and people (known as 'caserolazos' – pot-bangers) demonstrated against the economic chaos, leaving more dead and wounded. After Menem and allegations about corruption, came Duhalde and then De La Rua, the President who was more a victim than perpetrator of the failed policies. He ignominiously escaped the violence and demonstrations, late one afternoon, by helicopter (reminiscent of scenes of the last days of Saigon). The legacy of the western-inspired, IMF and World Bank economic development policies, debt and weapons sales was tragic.

The World Bank and IMF, partners in the quasi-development theory, used loan conditionality, firstly in Chile, to get their way in reforming pension systems. Subsequently, this was also used in Eastern Europe (Mueller, 2004). Overall, 68 countries were 'assisted' in their pension 'reforms' by over 200 World Bank loans 'now considered, even by the Bank itself, to have been a failure' (Hall, 2007, p. 156). The bodies of pensioners in Buenos Aires were photographed after hanging themselves in public when their pensions were cut. The *New York Times* asked if the rate of pensioner suicides was abnormal (*New York Times*, November 17, 1992; 'The Days Dwindle Down to Poverty and Suicide'). Some question! Presumably if it were below average for annual pensioner euthanasia, the World Bank and/or IMF policies would be judged an improvement.

The pensions disaster and the weapons triumph

The seminal publication by the World Bank was *Averting the Old Age Crisis: Policies to Protect the Old* AND *Promote Economic Growth*, World Bank, 1994 (Estelle James, coordinator, their emphasis). It sums up perfectly the World Bank economic development theory of the time. It is riddled with misleading, confused and tendentious arguments and data, arguing for privatisation solutions based on a tenuous theory of market development. It equates stock market growth with economic development (review in Minns 1996). Further supposition suggests that public sector schemes provide lower returns, while the author determines US states' schemes as private, thereby manipulating the definitions and data to her advantage.

The European model of welfare never entered their heads as an option because they were driven by their own theory of *private* pensions being key to economic growth, and hence the subtitle of their seminal book of 1994, *Policies to Protect the Old AND Promote Economic Growth* – a strange juxtaposition of ideas, both of which failed by any measure. James has responded to critics and, in 2007, disingenuously accused many of not having read her work, and claimed that she never advocated the Chilean model. One random quote from the above publication will suffice:

> *Nowhere has the influence of the Chilean experiment been felt more strongly than in Latin America. During the debt and fiscal crises of the 1980s, Latin America's pension schemes became seriously underfunded ... As the region entered the 1990s, the movement to privatise pensions gained momentum, urged on by the success of Chile.* (p. 276; further plaudits for the Chilean scheme elsewhere, particularly p. 212).

Followed by:

> *Although many have accused the book of directing policymakers to copy Chile's plan, those who have read* Averting the Old Age Crisis *know this is not the case.* (James in Kay and Sinha, 2008, p.165).

But we must move on.

The pension reforms in the geographical expansion of the privatized pension systems were assisted by US-backed dictatorships in the case of South America (recently acknowledged by James), and later in former communist dictatorships in Central and Eastern Europe through debt conditionality. Democracy appears to have been irrelevant. The power of subversion and debt was paramount in the establishment of welfare reform, involving billions of dollars of business and profit. The system is plagued by corporate financial self-interest and the extension of US hegemony in the definition of social and national security, however we

Table 6
US Companies and Private Pensions Management in South America.

Insurance Companies	Metropolitan Life and New York Life	Argentina
	Aetna	Peru and Chile
	American International Group	Argentina, Chile and Peru
Banks	Bankers Trust	Chile
	Bank of America	Peru
	Bank Boston	Argentina
	Citibank	Argentina, Chile and Peru

want to dress this up in the supposed anonymity of robotic 'globalisation'. Table 6 shows the US financial firms which benefited from the privatisation of pensions in South America. Fund managers received up to 30% commission, which is an extraordinary amount.

In summary, weapons for pensions take two forms. Firstly in the South American case, state pensions could be decimated to pay the enormous debt, a major part of which was used to buy weapons (in Argentina, two-thirds[4]). From 1974 to 1984, the share of Third World military spending by Latin America rose from 10 to 12 %, while the 'debt service ratio' increased from 13% to 53.2% between 1970 to 1982 (SIPRI Yearbook 1984, pp 95-96). The slow decimation of pensions could be called a coincidence, and the introduction of various private solutions just sensible housekeeping to improve economic growth. I leave the reader to judge.

Secondly, and relatedly, the privatisation of pensions in the face of the old age 'crisis' helps in the onward march of the private solution to welfare, and is a crucial factor in the support of fickle stock markets (Minns, 2001), the real point of privatisation. But Robert Holzmann (Director of the Social Protection Department at the World Bank) declares that there is unconvincing evidence as to whether they have even done that, especially in the exemplar of Chile. He concludes that it is time to move on to Central and Eastern Europe. (Holzmann, 1997, pp. 16 and 214).

To boil things down about the business of death, pensioners lost, the arms industry won. Pensioners helped pay for the odious debt, which should not have been repaid in the first place. Let us continue to make connections between subjects we are taught are not connected.

Recommendations

(a) The World Bank (US), BAE Systems (UK), Aerospatiale (France), Israeli Aerospace and Israeli Military Industries (Israel), Lockheed Martin (US), Boeing (US), Agusta Westland Helicopters (UK/Italy), Bell Helicopters (US), Steyr (Austria), Dassault (France), Fairchild (US), Raytheon (US), Euromissile (France), Panhard (France) should recompense the pensioners who paid substantially for their products. In 2006 the top ten arms manufacturers made \$12.3 trillion profits. The companies listed above made \$9.5 trillion.

(b) The UN Security Council, which presided over this and did nothing, should also commence discussions about reparations in its alleged concern for world prosperity and peace. Now that the failed experiment of reducing state pensions and promoting private ones is seen to have failed, this could be a way of reconstructing the 'traditional' model of pensions provision which was undermined in the cold war and variously used to pay for odious debt.

Notes

1 'Odious debt' is defined as debt incurred by 'underdeveloped' countries and misspent on arms or repression of the population. It does not serve the interest of the people and is used to strengthen a regime's position. The lenders are said to have committed a hostile act against the people and cannot expect the nation, having freed itself of the regime, to assume these 'odious' debts. (Definitions on various websites, eg Jubilee USA Network, and IMF on Odious Debt). Also see Adams, 1993.

2 The final part of this dedication and introduction is to certain individuals. Leonie Henriette Duquet, a French nun, age 61, Esther Ballestrino de Carreaga, 59, Maria Eugenia Poncede Bianco, 52, both of the latter were Mothers of May Square searching for their children, and Angela Auad, 28, human rights worker, all killed in 1977 by the Navy militia, condoned by the United States. The reason for my special reference is that what remained of their tortured and violated bodies was discovered in 2005 and interred in my local churchyard of Santa Cruz in San Cristobal, Buenos Aires. Its priests, Carlos Mugica, Monsenor Angelelli and Monsenor Romero were taken away in 1974, 1976 and 1980 respectively. They were not seen again. Also to Jaqueline Paulette Droully Yurich, murdered 30 October 1974, and Marcello Eduardo Salinas Eytel, 31 October 1974, Chileans, both of whom have plaques in the Peace Garden next to the Imperial War Museum in south London close to where I live in London. An interesting juxtaposition.

3 In the film/movie entitled *Lord of War* (apparently based on a true story) the arms dealer played by Nicholas Cage is advised by one of his sidekicks that there was an embargo on the export of helicopter gunships. Cage winces and proclaims that in the manifest they will be declared as 'rescue' helicopters. In

the sanitised version of the import records that I have there is an item called 'utility' helicopters.

4 We shall probably never know the exact proportion because many of the imports were illegal ('importaciones no registrades'). The debt was also used to build the infrastructure for the 1978 World Cup which Argentina controversially won – a useful propaganda stunt – and for the 'autopistas' which fly over Buenos Aires, under one of which was one of the most notorious detention centres, the 'Club Atletico'.

Bibliography

Adams, Patricia (1993) *Deudas Odiosas (Odious Debt), Un Legado de Insensatez Economica y Saqueo Ambiental (Loose Lending, Corruption and the Environmental Legacy),* Planeta Tierra., Buenos Aires.

Blackburn, Robin (2006) *Age Shock: How Finance is Failing Us,* Verso.

Calloni, Stella (1999) *Los Anos del Lobo: Operacion Condor; Kissinger, Pinochet, Stroessner, Banzer, Mason, Massera,* Ediciones Continente, Buenos Aires.

Gilbert, Bentley B (1966) *The Evolution of National Insurance in Great Britain; The Origins of the Welfare State,* Michael Joseph, London.

Gilbert, Bentley B (1970) *British Social Policy, 1914-1939,* Batsford, London.

Goni, Uki (2003) *The Real Odessa; How Peron Brought the Nazi War Criminals to Argentina,* Granta, London.

Gonzales, Gustavo (2004-2005) Pension Reforms hit women hard.' *Third World Economics,* December- January. based on a UN study of pension privatisation in Latin America, *Pension Systems in Latin America; A Gender Analysis,* ECLAC, Santiago.

Hall, Anthony (2007) 'Social Policies in the World Bank; Paradigms and Challenges', *Global Social Policy,* Vol 7, no 2, August.

Holzmann, Robert (1997) 'Pension Reform, Financial Market Development and Economic Growth: Preliminary Evidence from Chile, *IMF Working Paper, WP/96/94.*

Kay, Stephen J, and Sinha, Tapen, eds (2008) *Lessons from Pension Reform in the Americas,* Oxford University Press.

Kindleburger, Charles (1996) *Manias, Panics and Crashes; A History of Financial Crises,* Wiley, New York.

Klein, Naomi (2007) *The Shock Doctrine,* Penguin, London.

Madrid, Raul (2003) *Retiring the State; Politics of Pension Privatisation in Latin America and Beyond,* Stanford.

Menjivar, C. and Rodriguez, N. eds. (2005) *When States Kill; Latin America, the US, and the Technologies of Terror,* University of Texas Press, Austin.

Minns, Richard (1996) 'The Political Economy of Pensions', *New Political Economy,* Vol. 1, no. 3, November.

Minns, Richard (2001) *'The Cold War in Welfare; Stock Markets versus Pensions.* Verso, London and New York.

Minns, Richard (2006) 'The Mothers of May Square', *Soundings,* Issue 33, Summer.

Minns, Richard (2007) '"Estafa": Dictatorship, debt, weapons, in Argentina – An alternative perspective on pension "reform" in Latin America,' *Pensions, An International Journal,* Vol 12, no. 4, September.

Mount, Graeme (2002) *Chile and the Nazis; From Hitler to Pinochet,* Black Rose Books, Montreal.

Mueller, Katharina (2004) 'The Political Economy of Pension Reform in Central and Eastern Europe', in *Reforming Public Pensions; Sharing the Experience of Transition and OECD Countries*, ed. Peter Whitfield, OECD, Paris.

Paul, Susanna, S and Paul, James, A (1995) 'The World Bank and the Attack on Pensions in the Global South', *International Journal of Health Services*, Vol 25, no 4, December.

Rein, Raanan (2003) *Argentina, Israel and the Jews; Peron, the Eichmann Capture and After,* University Press, Maryland.

The Crisis

Oskar Lafontaine

Oskar Lafontaine was President of the German Bundesrat. He was the SPD's candidate for Federal Chancellor in 1990, when he was attacked with a knife and badly hurt. In September 1998 he became Federal Minister of Finance and resigned the following March. In 2005, he left the SPD and founded the Left Party. He is now joint Chairman of The Left (Die Linke). We reprint some excerpts from his comments about the current political crisis.

In October 2008, Oskar Lafontaine responded to a statement in the Bundestag by Federal German Finance Minister Peer Steinbrück. We print some excerpts from what he said.

'I think the term "financial market crisis" does not adequately describe the crisis we are talking about today. In our opinion this is not an economic crisis but rather a crisis of the intellectual and moral orientation of western industrialised societies.'

Responding to the interjection by a CDU/CSU MP that 'This is communism', Lafontaine said 'how pathetic. I must repeat that. A colleague shouted "This is communism". The Finance Minister just said it was necessary to regulate. Does this mean a communist is seated on the government bench? Don't be ridiculous. The whole world recognises now that regulation is necessary in the international financial markets. And you defame or discredit the demand for regulation as communism. It's really hard to believe.

I'd now like to raise a few issues on the question of what needs to be done. First, an issue, you Minister, did not speak about. We are convinced – let me repeat this for my party – that the current system of exchange rates is completely wrong as it tempts people to speculate, and that a proposal that has been on the table for more than 20 years should be considered, namely stabilising the exchange rates of the key currencies which nowadays also include the Chinese currency. What matters are target zones, which have been demanded internationally for many years. Nobel Prize laureate Robert Mundell demanded them again recently in an interview with *Frankfurter Allgemeine Zeitung*. As long as you don't raise this subject you won't do anything about the first slump after the collapse of the Bretton Woods system.

The second issue concerns regulation of international capital movements. This is what Mr Schmidt (former German Chancellor) meant. Twenty years ago he said that rules are needed, as in motor traffic, sea traffic and air traffic. Or take a speculator like Soros who said that since capital could flow into a small national economy within just a few months – that was the crisis in Thailand, then – there should at least be devices to stop the elusive capital from leaving the country overnight and ruining the entire national economy. The supervision of international capital movements is the second point I'd like to raise here.

The third demand is to dry up the tax havens. You don't really believe that you manage to sort out the international financial markets if many industrialised countries, tongue in cheek, hang on to their tax havens where money gets laundered and untaxed money keeps accumulating.

It is to be welcomed that at last it has dawned on people that the rating agencies must, at least, be controlled. We say the rating agencies belong under society's supervision. Just as it would not be advisable to leave licensing drugs to the pharmaceutical industry, it is of little merit to leave admission of financial products to the finance industry. This is unbelievable. It is commendable that it has, at least, been identified now.

Of course, we need international rules in supervising banks. They have been worked on for decades. Some improvements have been made. Yet, apparently, they have not sufficed; otherwise we would not have these undesirable developments now. Such rules only make sense if all adhere to them; this has been mentioned, to be fair.

Let's talk about individual responsibility. It's really wonderful to point at international financial regulation and not to accept one's own responsibility. I can support the speaker of the Free Democratic Party. You should have spoken about your own responsibility. I'd like to point out the coalition agreement demands exactly what you have criticised … Why don't you say anything about this? You have your part of the responsibility to accept.

The same goes, of course, for hedge funds, which were admitted by the previous government. After you identified the consequences of leverage effects, you should have done something to terminate hedge funds borrowing 40 Euros to the one Euro they own, thus causing disarray in entire national economies or companies. Why haven't you done anything? It really comes in handy to point at the United States, and say everything has been so terribly bad there. You have nobody to blame but yourself; this gives you enough to do Finance Minister. Face up to your own responsibility!'

In conclusion, Oskar Lafontaine said: 'We now witness that the formula of free market superiority has been driven into the ground, and that we are no longer subject to the control of international financial markets, but that those markets force us to make decisions due to misguided developments, decisions that are counterproductive, and which we did not intend to make because they result in big losses which nobody can foresee. We have learnt that the phrase "we cannot govern against the international financial markets" must be turned around: we must act against the international financial markets to get a handle on the system again, at last.'

Edward Carpenter Unsung Hero

Michael Barratt Brown

Michael Barratt Brown was founding principal of Northern College near Barnsley. Here he discusses Sheila Rowbotham's new book, Edward Carpenter: A Life of Liberty and Love, *(Verso, 2008).*

Sheila Rowbotham has completed her earlier studies of Edward Carpenter in *History Workshop Journal* (1977) and in *History Today* (1987) with a full-length biography. She has been able to draw on the large Carpenter Collection now in the Sheffield City Archive, but her research has extended world-wide to archives in London, Manchester, Leeds, Oxford, Cambridge, Texas, Syracuse, Ohio, Washington, Amsterdam, and New Zealand, and to interviews with anyone who personally knew Carpenter or had relatives who did. Sheila Rowbotham's present position as Professor of Labour and Gender History at Manchester University has enabled her to carry to completion this labour of love. And it is a splendid piece of work, beautifully written and engaged in her subject as only Sheila, with her feminist commitment and communal experience, as described in her autobiographical *Promise of a Dream*, could have achieved. For, this is not just a history; it contains profound reflections on the deep problems of personal and political choice that engage us in our own time.

There is practically no important issue which engages us today that Carpenter did not raise and throw new light upon just over a hundred years ago, and this applies most particularly for those of us involved in struggles to correct the continuing inequalities and injustices in society, which were Carpenter's chief concern. These issues range from environmental pollution, most disastrous before the smoke abatement acts in the poorer housing of the steel-making city of Sheffield, from which Carpenter fled to the surrounding countryside; to the oppression of women and of colonial peoples and their exclusion from equal opportunities in employment and remuneration; to the class structure in British society which holds back the majority of men and women, in Carpenter's day the vast majority, from receiving a complete education and enjoying the benefits, social, financial and cultural which such an education assures. Carpenter's response to these injustices was not only to throw himself into every campaign he could find and many which he generated himself – for slum clearance, for conservation in nature reserves, for recycling waste, for garden allotments, for women's suffrage, for birth control and legal abortion, for prison reform, for universal education, for animal rights, and for his particular brand of socialism – of which more later.

To advance these causes Carpenter took on a prodigiously heavy programme of lecturing on the whole range of his concerns and of writing – books and pamphlets – giving carefully argued support to advocates of these causes, often combined with generous financial assistance. He everywhere sought out friends and associates to join with him in these endeavours. But Carpenter did not confine his activities to intellectual work. He tried always to practise what he preached. He did not eat meat. He built a simple house in the country a few miles outside Sheffield with enough space for visitors and enough land to grow his own fruit and vegetables and keep chickens. A stream ran through the garden and Carpenter's day began with a 'skinny dip' in the water at all times of the year. He made his own sandals and went for long walks through the local valleys and onto the moors, and took his friends and visitors with him. Provisions and furnishings were brought by hand cart from the shops in nearby Chesterfield.

How does it come, then, that Carpenter, who was a pioneer of so many progressive causes, remains unsung? His circle of friends was not only wide but influential, and their names well known, including not only his guru, Walt Whitman, and Oscar Wilde, but John Ruskin, Bertrand Russell, E.M.Forster, Havelock Ellis, Bernard Shaw, Evelyn Sharp, H.M.Hyndman, Olive Schreiner, Roger Fry, Miles Malleson, Hugh Massingham, Henry Nevinson, Fenner Brockway, Annie Besant, George Lansbury, Hugh Dalton, Charles Trevelyan, and Ramsay MacDonald. But none of these attended his funeral, in 1929 at the age of 85. He had been ill for some years before the end and had fallen out of touch with many of these famous people, but this cannot explain the disappearance of Carpenter from the histories. Most of the issues he fought for, against fierce prejudice and vested interest, have become commonly accepted parts of our lives (the exception is, perhaps, his rejection of vaccination and vivisection).This cannot quite explain the neglect.

There are two or three possible explanations for this neglect. The first must be that many people felt, and some may continue to feel, uncomfortable about his blatant homosexuality. His 'coming out' in a long-term male partnership, and many sexual adventures throughout his life with eligible young men, after some years of concealment, was very courageous, and sometimes dangerous, but was calculated (deliberately so) not to attract everyone. The second reason for neglect is that Carpenter was not a 'joiner'. He supported but did not join progressive causes. He never joined the Independent Labour Party (ILP) or the Labour Party, which were formed during his lifetime, and he never joined a trade union, although Sheffield was full of them. So, he does not appear in their histories, along with Keir Hardie, Tom Mann, Bob Williams or Ernest Bevin. The third reason is Carpenter's mysticism. This is a much more complex matter, which few people are prepared to understand. He was not only interested in Hindoo thought, through a Sinhalese friend from Cambridge days, but saw the marriage of the soul, in a mystical sense, and the body, in a richly physical sense, as the basis for living and for understanding life. It was all part of his belief in the human need to return to nature, and to remove all artificial impediments to living the simple life. It is well summarised by Sheila Rowbotham in 'Carpenter's vision of the new order in touch with nature and satisfying the heart – free from domination and imbued with the values of association while allowing space for self expression, sex and the inner life ...'

Hard though it is today to understand Carpenter's thinking about the emancipation of the body and the spirit, as anyone who has tried to read his great tone poem 'Towards Democracy' will have found, his absolute insistence on preserving individual thought and choice in a planned socialist economy, something which the Soviet leaders neglected, has a very modern resonance. His determination to retain his individualism was part of his personal pride as a man, and a man's man, and was reflected in his dress and old fashioned courteous behaviour, which so endeared him to his many friends. Roger Fry's painting of Carpenter, which is reproduced in this book, shows a tall man with beard neatly trimmed, meticulously dressed in a long tailored coat, polished shoes, upturned shirt collar and florid cravat. He affected a silk kummerbund with his regular everyday tweed jacket and sandals. This is not the apparel of the simple country worker, which he liked to present to the world. It reveals the remarkable complexity of the man – philosopher, teacher, poet, activist, organiser, musician, market gardener, mystic, and withal a lover of men in every sense.

Carpenter's attitude to the 1914-18 War says it all. He was not opposed to the war, as were most of his friends and associates, such as Russell and Forster, Brockway and Olive Schreiner. He came from a military family. Many of his relatives were high-ranking soldiers or sailors. He was too old to be called up himself. His partner was not, but was rejected on health grounds. Carpenter's position was much more complex than these superficial reasons suggest. He saw destruction in nature as a necessary preparation for regeneration. With D.H. Lawrence he therefore saw 'hate and conflict' acting as a crucial catalyst for change, leading to a new social order. In Russia the 1914-18 War did just that, but the new order did not embrace the sort of collectivism Carpenter believed in. What he did oppose most vehemently was military conscription, since this denied to the individual the right to make his own choice. So he supported the No Conscription Fellowship, of which Russell was the chairman. He was unsympathetic to both religious and political pacifism. That left a sort of humanistic pacifism, which avoided the stark choices such as Carpenter always shied away from.

Carpenter's attitude to Quakerism interests me greatly because my father was a very active member of the Society of Friends and had a great admiration for Carpenter. At an early age I was given *Towards Democracy* to read. It was a long time afterwards that I cottoned on to the homosexual references. Walt Whitman was one of my father's favourite poets along with the Quaker Whittier. It was therefore a great surprise to find no references to Quakers in the exhaustive index to Sheila Rowbotham's book. In fact there are three references: one is to a Quaker neighbour of Carpenter's in Derbyshire, Mrs. Doncaster, a member of the steel-making family firm in Sheffield; the second is more relevant: Carpenter is quoted saying in 1915 that he did not think 'peace societies … and Quaker and Tolstoyan preachments were adequate to plumb such depths' as the 'emotions, habits, instincts, myths' which war engendered. A few pages later, 'more radical Quakers' are referred to, talking about social reconstruction after the war. This was following lectures by Russell, which had brought him and Forster and D.H. Lawrence briefly together. That was all, the snide reference to 'preachments'. But in my memory many of our family's Quaker friends had for years adopted a simple lifestyle and speech, minimal furniture (but William Morris designed wallpaper and curtains), plain clothes with open neck shirts, tweed jackets and sandals, and their belongings (and vegetarian sandwiches) in a small rucksack. My father always wore a large broad brimmed hat. He had a cold bath every morning and, during his years in prison for anti-war activities, persuaded the warders to hose him down in the prison yard. We grew our own fruit and vegetables and went long walks, called rambles. Women had absolutely equal status with men in Quaker families and in Quaker business meetings. Non-procreative love making was accepted and cherished. The Quaker faith was not really Christian, but a kind of mystical humanism.

Now the question I am bound to ask is which was dominant, Quakerism or Carpenterism? The near absence of reference to Quakerism in Carpenter's many writings and activities suggests a parallel development. But the Quaker influences must have been strong. The poet Whittier was a Quaker, Bertrand Russell's first wife, Alys Pearsall-Smith, was a Quaker, the mother of William Temple, president of the Workers Educational Association, was a Quaker, the Adult School Movement was a Quaker stronghold. The Quaker chocolate companies – Cadbury's, Rowntree's, Fry's and Terry's – and the brewers – Truman, Hanbury & Buxton – were at their highest influence at the turn of the century, through the *News Chronicle* and the banks – Barclays, Lloyds, Midland, National Provincial. Even Marie Stopes was the daughter of a Quaker brewer. Nearer Carpenter's home, there were not only the Sheffield Quaker businessmen, Doncasters and Coopers, but also the Brayshaws and other Quaker lawyers and lecturers. Most of the leading members of the No Conscription Fellowship, like my father, were Quakers. In India Gandhi's close friend and adviser, Horace Alexander, was a Quaker. So many of the organisations Carpenter supported and lectured to were financed by Quaker philanthropists. Perhaps, that is why he did not wish to acknowledge their influence.

What remains to be said is a final word about Carpenter's socialism. The point has already been made that it was based on a romantic individualism, to which collectivist ideas had to be adapted. Carpenter favoured nationalisation, most especially of the mines, but on the basis of guild socialism and not of state ownership. In 1910 Carpenter took the chair at a mass meeting in the Albert Hall, organised by the Social Democratic Party and the ILP, to welcome Tom Mann back from Australia. Mann's syndicalism particularly attracted Carpenter, who had high hopes of industrial unionism developing into industrial syndicalism, on lines that G.D.H.Cole was to argue for intellectual as well as for manual workers, but extending syndicalism to the making of beautiful things, beautiful clothes and, thus, beautiful people. Unfortunately, it was never very clear how such beauty fitted into Carpenter's new social order. Bertrand Russell had to spend a whole night in the attic of his young girlfriend, the actress Colette O'Niel, alias the Hon Constance Malleson (née Annesley), who became Russell's most long lasting love, disabusing her of her infatuation with Carpenter's romantic idealism. But, many socialists then and now must recognise the place of love and liberty in any social order moving 'towards democracy'. There is so much in Carpenter's life, and in Sheila Rowbotham's evocation of it, to make us think about what we should do with our lives and how we could make them more productive.

The gist of Carpenter's message is a refutation of the concept of economic man making rational decisions in response to the pressures of authorities and markets. A whole-ist approach is required to human organisation and behaviour which allows for the rich diversity of individual human tastes and emotions, and should indeed encourage such diversity. In practical terms this means cooperative organisation, workers' control, decentralised government and popular community participation – in effect, development from the bottom upwards in place of the top-downwards rule by employers and state authorities. This was a hard enough programme to advocate in Carpenter's day, although his efforts – organising groups of free thinkers and working with the unions, especially the coal miners, as well as writing and lecturing - did have some success. In our own time of giant international corporations and combinations of states' powers in a United States, a European Union, a multi-state China or India, it must seem well nigh impossible. Yet Carpenter's dream remains a very real aspiration in the national movements of many peoples sharing common historic experiences, languages and cultures. The building of such movements within the limits of our shared planet remains the challenge for us all.

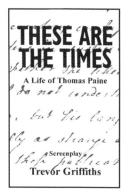

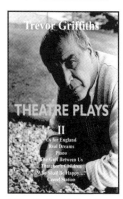

Unite

London & Eastern Region
Woodberry, 218 Green Lanes,
London, N4 2HB

London Labour Party Conference

**Labour and Unite
working together to ensure
no BNP win in the Euro-elections**

Steve Hart - Regional Secretary

P: 020.8800.4281   F: 020.8802.8388

www.unitetheunion.com

Reviews

Espiocracy

John Le Carré, *A Most Wanted Man*, Hodder & Stoughton, 350 Pages, cloth ISBN 9780340977064, £18.99

James Rubin, during his brief and ill-starred career as an 'anchor' man for Sky News, defined 'extraordinary rendition' as an operation when the authorities in the country from which the US was rendering its captives didn't know what was happening. When the authorities did know what was going on, that was simply 'rendition' as usual. Madeleine Albright's junior at the Department of State during President Clinton's second term seemed to have some direct experience of rendition and how it is practised by United States agencies.

According to Rubin's definition, the pending rendition of Issa and Abdullah, innocent and 'five per cent bad' respectively, at the conclusion of John Le Carré's new novel would appear to be not at all 'extraordinary'. Their snatch in Hamburg is facilitated by regional and Federal German agencies, even to the extent of disabling the plans of Günther Bachmann, experienced spook, who thought he had the support of German foreign intelligence.

Bachmann contends that Hamburg was 9/11's second ground zero. Mohamed Atta, who flew one of planes into New York's Twin Towers on that sunny September morning, came from Cairo to Hamburg in 1992 to continue his architectural studies. In due course, he joined with others to plan the attacks on the United States. How had German intelligence failed to stop this? The answer lies in part in the failure to recruit influential persons in the Muslim community, according to Bachmann. Recruiting and running agents is what he is good at. He has demonstrated this in Beirut and elsewhere, although not always to the satisfaction of his superiors in the 'espiocracy', as le Carré styles it. But such skill is no longer highly valued or appreciated by the German intelligence operation, it seems. Instead, they increasingly take their cue from the United States agencies, assisted closely by SIS, the United Kingdom's Special Intelligence Service. This is 'justice from the hip' for those who 'kill Americans'. Will that change under President Obama?

All the hallmarks of a good Le Carré romp are here: breakneck pace, gathering tension, plots within plots. There is the Red Army colonel who, in the 1980s, sensed which way the wind was blowing and joined the SIS payroll. He was a 'cultured' Russian with a penchant for Tchaikovsky and Turgenev, which he has passed on to his confused and rootless son, Issa, whose Chechen mother was killed by her own family because of her relationship with the colonel. Here are echoes of Le Carrés 'cultured' and clever spooks of Soviet times, whom George Smiley seemed to admire somehow, although he knew he shouldn't.

By contrast, the British spooks are bereft of redeeming features. The 'sulphurous' older generation (John Scarlett?), who learned their trade during the Cold War, is giving way to young men from the English Midlands who utter the most direct threats to get their way. No charm at all.

Almost every character in *The Most Wanted Man* is trying it on. Annabel Richter, Issa's young German lawyer who works with refugees, is recruited by Bachmann. The Scottish Banker, Brue, sees in Annabel his own somewhat estranged daughter, and yet somehow falls for her, too. He is recruited by SIS, following in his own father's footsteps. *Fathers and Children*, the title of Turgenev's novel about nihilism, which is often mistranslated as 'Fathers and Sons', sums up a key part of the energy of Le Carré's twenty-first novel, which is dedicated to his grandchildren, born and unborn. May the legacy continue to grow.

Tony Simpson

Denying Denial

Stan Cox, *Sick Planet: Corporate Food and Medicine*, Pluto Press, 220 pages, paperback ISBN 978 07453 2740 2, £14.99

Stan Cox is described on the cover of this book as a senior scientist at the Land Institute in Salina, Kansas. He worked for the US Department of Agriculture from 1984 to 1996. He has a PhD in plant genetics.

The theme of his book is ecological sustainability. The author's broad conclusion is that profit-driven market economics is leading to environmental degradation, ill health, and resource depletion. The detailed studies include the distorted priorities of US health care, the 'disease mongering' of pharmaceutical companies worldwide, the energy cost of chemical fertilisers, and the irreconcilability of growth in energy consumption and population with finite resources of fossil fuel.

India is rich in the renewable energy sources of sunlight and wind, and the author sees the replacement of fossil fuels with such sources, combined with less use of chemical fertiliser and better water management, as a way of responding to climate change, which he finds has already resulted in reduced rainfall in 12 of 36 regions in India. He describes a recently suspected effect of industrial pollution of the atmosphere in India and elsewhere where the formation of 'brown clouds' limits the evaporation of water from the oceans and, while to some extent countering global warming, produces less rainfall. Also with some personal experience of India he describes the links between local government corruption and the toxic pollution of already deprived areas resulting in what he calls 'ecological sacrifice zones' and 'Bhopal in slow motion'.

Although the subtitle of the book, *Corporate Food and Medicine,* suggests a narrower field, it soon becomes clear that the author's concern is the degradation of the planet, not least by resource depletion. He asks how can an increasing population be fed when the oceans are fished not only for food but also for fuel and fertilizer.

When writing the book the author must have been aware that the strategy of 'Shock and Awe', the 'Operation Iraqi Freedom', the 'Operation Enduring Freedom', and other interventions in Middle East affairs were connected with oil supplies. The rapid rise of energy prices, the fear of recession, the mortgage-credit crisis, and the collapse of some of the world's leading banks probably occurred while the book was with the publisher, and if he were writing a post-script Stan Cox would surely want to know how the threats to attack Iran also affected the price of oil, the energy futures market, and the subsequent train of events. It is impolitic to mention the war, but it remains necessary. Much of that is implied, and what the book does focus on is the sustainability of capitalism itself. Short references to Kant and Marx provide the hints that this is coming, and that some of his American readers may need some preparation for it.

Economic growth is essential to capitalism because enterprises that are not growing are vulnerable to collapsing share value, loss of credit worthiness, and insolvency. We then have to work out how 'sustainable growth' is to be achieved alongside the targets now being set for an 80% reduction in carbon emissions by 2050 only to *mitigate* the economic effects of climate change.

In the final chapter of the book the author speculates briefly how capitalism may be changed. A refusal to be ruled by a tiny class of owners is essential, and he expects that will bring 'terrible retaliation'. The author envisages other changes that may modify capitalism, looking particularly, but not too hopefully, to Europe. He offers that '… to believe that the Soviet road is the only way to a post-capitalist society is to have no imagination', and quotes sympathetically the ecosocialist view that 'capitalism is working about as well as any pyramid scheme does before it goes bust'. What prescience!

Stan Cox does not claim to have an answer, but he suggests that 'stiff regulation' of business, more worker ownership worldwide, green taxes, the enforcement of anti-trust laws, and the redistribution of wealth will put useful pressure on the system, and that many small co-operative initiatives will be needed. (Better regulation hasn't really been tried because 'regulatory reform' still translates to deregulation, and only recently a committee of MPs proposed the deregulation of the insurance market!) The highest obstacle, and an essential first step, the author says, is to give up on denial.

Christopher Gifford

Neoliberalism Dissected

Jim Stanford, *Economics for Everyone – A Short Guide to the Economics of Capitalism*, Pluto Press, 360 pages, ISBN 9780745327501 (paperback), £12.99, ISBN 9780745327518 (hardback), £40.00

Commencing with the maxim 'never trust an economist with your job', Jim Stanford sets out to demystify and free economics from the hands of academic obscurantism, or, as he calls it, 'complicated technical mumbo-jumbo'. This is an extremely laudable ambition and a very necessary one, given the assumed certainties of much of the 'informed' economic opinion with which we are daily bombarded from the media's pundits and politicians alike, perhaps a little more chastened of late given our 'credit crisis'. Even Mr. Greenspan has had second thoughts. The author is a Canadian trade unionist and economist, working for the Canadian Auto Workers Union, so I think it is pretty safe to make the assumption that he understands the realities of working life in an advanced industrial society in thrall to the ideological diktats of neoliberalist economics, and seeks to bring genuine enlightenment. In fact the whole book could be read as a highly successful criticism of neo-liberalism in areas where it claims some success, in particular, investment, global development and wealth creation.

The book exudes a practical and clear style taking the reader logically through what is complex territory without managing to either befuddle or induce narcolepsy — quite an achievement for a book on economics. In fact, I don't think there is one algebraic formula within it, and the various diagrams illustrating the circulatory nature of economic processes are clear and informative. Throughout the book pithy illustrations lighten the text and provide a humorous lift, very much an improvement on the usual economic textbook illustrations of death by a thousand supply and demand curves! For those who wish to take their studies further there is a dedicated website connected to the book (*www.economicsforeveryone.com*), which would be of obvious help.

Sandford takes us through the usual territory: a brief insight into economic history and its present day evolution into capitalism, followed by a tour of the basics of capitalism, its driving forces and inherent contradictions. We move on to the functioning of capitalism and its complexities, covering, for example, investment and growth, the environment, banking, finance and the stock market, globalisation, inequality, the role of government, and the important question of capitalism's ups and downs. With regard to the latter, the present economic crisis would have possibly made a difference to its emphasis in the book, but certainly not to its overall content or conclusion. As one would expect, the present recession confirms many of the ideas put forward. *Economics for Everyone*, of course, by its very nature covers a vast area of human knowledge and action, and serves as an admirable introduction to the subject, but it also manages to serve as an active agitational text.

It is clear is that the book is meant to inspire practical activity, as well as elucidating the niceties of economics. Clearly, one of the primary target audiences for the text is the trade union activist, if not ordinary members, and, pleasingly, the author is in no doubt of the importance of a vibrant, forceful and numerically large trade union movement. This comes in the context of the precipitous fall in trade union membership in the advanced industrial nations since the 1970s. For, to quote the author on the importance of trade unions:

'No society without strong and effective unions has ever achieved truly mass prosperity. The degree of unionisation is one of the most important factors determining wage levels, the incidence of poverty, and hours of work.'

The concluding part of *Economics for Everyone* is one of the most stimulating, touching as it does on the question of the overall evaluation of capitalism, its possible improvement, or abolition. Through the novel mechanism of a checklist the author acknowledges the successes of capitalism in terms of innovation and choice and, of course, significant progress in terms of prosperity for some, examining these factors in the context of the failures of Soviet socialism and social democracy. (In this context I fear his opinion may be a little too northern hemispherically-centred, but, of course, there's always the growth success of China to take into account). The thrust of his closing argument seems to be that we should fight 'to make our respective countries more like the Nordic variant of capitalism and less like the Anglo-Saxon version'. He couples this with an admirable 'reformers shopping list', which we could add to or amend in the light of our particular national peculiarities. He admits that 'Socialists have no obvious roadmap to guide their quest for a fundamentally more just and democratic economy', so maybe the main thing is to begin the journey, and this book will serve as a useful practical guide.

John Daniels

The Economics of Inequality

Polly Toynbee & David Walker, *Unjust Rewards*, Granta, 256 pages, ISBN 9781847080936, £12.99

This book contains all the statistics on inequality in the UK that you would expect from David Walker, and the informative interviews you would want from Polly Toynbee. The latter range from the very wealthy to the very poor. The former reveal an astonishing ignorance of, and lack of concern, for the lives of their less advantaged fellow human beings, and the latter an exceptional lack of anger or hope concerning their condition. Both of these responses suggest great difficulties in making any correction in these disparities. The scale of the inequalities revealed by the statistics is appalling. The earnings of top company executives can be anything up to a thousand times the minimum wage, and that wage provides less than two-thirds of what a family of four needs to live on. Excuses for such high salaries and extra compensation range from fear that the best brains might otherwise leave the country, to a belief that extra pay is needed to get the best out of people. There is no evidence for these assumptions, and the argument is applied only to the rich and not to the poor. About one-fifth of the UK population have household incomes below the official poverty line. That is two-thirds of the general standard of living for thirteen million people, most of the adults being in work. For the children it means no toys, no holidays, an unhealthy diet apart from school meals, and little incentive to study.

What is most disturbing in the statistical picture is that under 'New' Labour the gap between the rich and the poor has been widening. There may have been some narrowing up to 2004, but since then the rich have been getting richer and the poor actually poorer. It is not only the super-rich who have been gaining – executive pay rising by up to 30% to 40% a year while public sector pay rises have been held down by government to 2%. The Government's aim was to end child poverty, as the Scandinavians had done. Of the 3.4million children in poverty in 1998, the number was down by 600,000 in 2006, and nobody expects that the aim of halving the total will be achieved by 2010, particularly after the effects of the current financial crisis. Child tax credits have done most to alleviate child poverty, but they often mean that employers rely on this supplement to keep down the wages they pay. The Sure Start programme of child centres is probably the most imaginative and effective way of ending child poverty, and at the same time raising the educational level of the one-third of the population which is innumerate and can barely read and write. But there are only very few centres so far, and £7.2 billion a year would be needed to make them universal. The UK spends only 0.5% of GDP on the under fives, compared with 1.0% in France and 2.0% in Denmark, and in the new financial crisis such provision would hardly be a priority.

Even the middle classes can be shown to have been suffering. To take one example, a place at a private boarding school, which would almost certainly guarantee a place at Oxford or Cambridge or at one of the other more prestigious universities, now costs around £20,000 a year, excluding uniforms and books. Most of Middle England, according to focus groups, would be prepared to pay more taxes for education, but that was before the financial crisis. Toynbee and Walker, in the last chapter of the book on what needs to be done, recommend a large increase in taxes on the rich, and especial attention to taxing those who claim not to be domiciled in the UK, and employ other means of tax evasion in tax havens, all this combined with generally much more transparency about incomes, so as to develop what they call a 'pro-tax culture'. They suggest a property tax and strengthening inheritance taxes, with increased earmarking of taxes to benefit the poor, and laws to strengthen equal pay for women. All this must appear totally utopian in the light of the current financial crisis and the means proposed by the Government for bailing out the banks. But it suggests what might be done if a movement could be built to end Government's bribes to the rich and replace this with benefits for all, and especial protection for the poor. Such a policy would need to be based on an understanding that has escaped Toynbee and Walker's study of injustice, and that is that increasing inequalities have always been the cause of capitalist crises, the poor majority becoming increasingly unable to buy what is produced, and the rich with consequently no incentive to invest their capital in productive activity, choosing instead financial speculation.

Michael Barratt Brown

Asiatic Mode

Joseph Needham, *Science and Civilisation in China, Volume 5, Chemistry and Chemical Technology, Part 11: Ferrous Metallurgy* by Donald B. Wagner, Cambridge University Press, 478 pages, £120

Joseph Needham, *Science and Civilisation in China, Volume 7, The Social Background, Part 2: General Conclusions and Reflections*, edited by K. G. Robinson, Cambridge University Press, 284 pages, ISBN 9780521087322, £84

Joseph Needham died in 1995, but now, well into the next Century, his great work still continues. The first two volumes of his titanic *History of Science and Civilisation in China* were conventional single volumes, albeit volumes of incredible density and profundity. But by now there are twenty-four separate volumes, which have been continuously emerging during half a century of progress. Volume 3 was the first to subdivide into three ponderous books. By the time that we reached Volume 5, on *Chemistry and Chemical Technology*, the subdivisions had rocketed ahead, and this text on *Ferrous Metallurgy* is the eleventh book in this volume.

It has been a long time in gestation. Needham asked Donald Wagner to collaborate in the *History* in the very early eighties, and work began in earnest in 1994, after much preliminary research. Wagner is not an uncritical follower of Needham, and he does not really think that Ferrous Metallurgy is a department of Chemical Technology. Neither does he follow the master in his appreciation of the social sciences, which he had deemed to be less than fully social and greatly less than fully scientific. But for all that, he is a worthy disciple of the great man, and his book is a splendid contribution to the Needham project.

My own interest in the technology of iron production was stimulated by Wu Dakun, the Chinese historian, who was a proponent of the Marxist schema of an Asiatic Mode of Production. Throughout his life he changed his opinion on this more than once, and indeed it remains rather an open question, having been dissected by Perry Anderson, among others. But by

1983 Wu contributed an essay to the little volume *Marxism in China* which we published in Spokesman. It was called *The Asiatic Mode of Production in History, as Viewed by Political Economy in its Broad Sense*. The first part of this essay concerns general questions about the views of Marx and Engels on a distinct Asiatic mode of production. It recapitulates the story, familiar to Western scholars, of the views of Marx and Engels as set out in the well-known *Contribution to the Critique of Political Economy*, in *Capital*, and elsewhere. But the second part concerns the applicability of these doctrines to actual Chinese history, from the dawn of the Iron Age onwards.

Wu Dakun maintains that in China, just as in Europe, iron ploughs transformed the system of farming, and introduced the Asiatic type of land tenure referred to by Marx. In a summary of his arguments, which shows quite remarkable conciseness as well as breadth of vision, Wu Dakun demonstrates the exceptional features which characterise Chinese evolution, and establish the institutions which later prevented the development of a native Chinese form of capitalism.

I was very privileged to meet with Wu Dakun at a peace conference in Beijing about a year later. I reminded him of a much earlier article he had contributed to the English journal, *Past and Present*, and I also asked him about his relationship with Joseph Needham.

I was surprised to learn that Wu Dakun himself had proposed to Needham that he should embark upon a history of Chinese sciences whilst both of them were working in Chungking during the Second World War. I later mentioned this conversation to Needham himself, who spoke most warmly of Wu Dakun. Together we agreed that it would be a good idea to organise a symposium on the asiatic mode of production or the historical dynamics of Asiatic societies, and to invite Wu Dakun to participate in it. It took a long time to find the means to arrange for such a meeting, but finally we did secure the resources with the help of a generous contribution from Ahmed Ben Bella, the founding President of Algeria, who told me that he had read the French translation of the first volume of Needham's magisterial work whilst he was under house arrest in Msila. Unfortunately, Wu Dakun was not, in the event, able to join us for this meeting, which was to be held in Needham's Institute in Cambridge.

It is a thousand pities that Wu Dakun is not available to tell us about his reaction to the touring exhibitions of the Terracotta Warriors, the funerary guardians of the grandiose tomb of the First Emperor of the Qin Dynasty. Popular history is now flourishing throughout Western Europe, tracing the despotic lineaments of that Emperor. But Wu Dakun asks many other serious questions about the role of iron technologies in the development of the economies of the Warring States, which go deeper than the shock and horror of despotism.

Some time later, I went back to China with Stuart Holland, on behalf of Neil Kinnock, the then Leader of the British Labour Party. We arranged various meetings with the Chinese Communist leadership, with a view to securing Chinese participation in a conference of the Socialist International on the themes of the Brandt Report on North-South development questions, in the preparation of which Stuart had played a significant role.

We were invited to meet with Qiao Shi, who had recently been appointed to the Politburo. He arranged a banquet in the Great Hall of the People, where we were surprised to find ourselves meeting with the British Ambassador. Stuart began to tease the Ambassador about the Mandarinate, and he became quite cross, because Mandarins were not then flavour of the month in China, even if the behaviour of modern leaders was sometimes reminiscent of earlier times. To shift the subject into a less contentious area, Qiao Shi turned to me, and asked me for my views on the part played by the development of iron technologies in the period of the Warring States. Evidently he must have been familiar with the fact that I had been involved in publishing the Wu Dakun paper, because that at that time furnished the sum total of my knowledge on this, to us, somewhat exotic subject.

The Chinese Communists did attend the meeting of the Socialist International on the Brandt Report in Peru, but shortly afterwards political crises in China changed all the personnel in the leadership, and Qiao Shi disappeared from the top table. My friend, Su Shaozhi, from his eminent position as Director of the Institute of Marxism, Leninism and Mao Tse-Tung Thought, was to find himself in exile.

Far away in Cambridge, I pursued the project for a symposium on the Historical Dynamics of Oriental Societies with Joseph Needham, and this took place in 1990.

Joseph Needham tells us in the first volume of his *History* that the State of Qin in Shantung was notable for two powerful reasons. It was a major source of salt, and it led the way in the working of iron. Iron had become known in China by 500 BC and the Qin's mastery of iron technologies gave it a pre-eminence 'which may well have been significant in their bid for power'.

As iron technologies prospered, 'we also enter the greatest period of intellectual development in ancient China. The "one hundred schools" of philosophers were at their height between 500 and 250 BC ... During this period academies of scholars were set up, the most famous being the Academy of the Gate of Chi (Chi-Hsia) at the Chhi capital.' Increased productivity with iron ploughs helped all the arts to prosper, not only those of war.

Donald Wagner can add a great deal to Needham's early insights, both here and in his pathbreaking collection of essays and lectures called *The Grand Titration*. Wagner does this from the archaeological record, which has burgeoned in recent years. He can trace the discovery of iron artefacts across the centuries; some of the findings from the minus eighth century are clearly made from cast iron while others are made from wrought iron. Whilst wrought iron came to China from the West, iron casting was a Chinese invention. A luxury iron dagger wrought with other metals was found in a royal tomb (in the northern part of Chu) dated to the end of the minus sixth century. But equally old iron implements for practical use have been found at another Chu settlement.

In the northern Chinese States, at this time, the production of bronze was concentrated in a few large centres, and developed into a high art, producing castings 'which are among the finest the world has known, even in modern times'. Because of the extreme scarcity of copper, the incentive to develop processes for casting iron became that much greater. The earlier cast iron implements so far discovered have been implement caps found in the minus fourth century and later. The original advantage of cast iron implements was that they were cheaper than bronze. But they were brittle, and 'for most purposes not a good material'.

It was not until the beginning of the minus third century that there is evidence for a widespread use of iron throughout China.

In minus three hundred China consisted of a group of 'Warring States', although one of these had begun to conquer some of the others. This process was to lead to the unification of the States in the Qin Empire (or Chin, or Chhin in the various transliterations used in the earlier Needham volumes). The Qin Empire consolidated itself in minus 220, creating a highly centralised administration and embarking upon very large-scale public works, such as the first Emperor's mausoleum, now famous for the Terracotta Army which guarded it, the Great Wall, a long distance road system, and centralised stores for the husbanding of grain.

The Qin Empire soon over-extended and gave rise to peasant uprisings which brought about its downfall and the establishment of a new Empire, the Han, in minus 206. It was the Han Empire which introduced a State monopoly in the salt and iron industries, bringing new possibilities for technical development.

Mencius, writing at the end of the minus fourth century, recorded a dialogue on the developing division of labour.

'Does Master Xu cook with a (metal) pot and a (earthenware) steamer?'
'Does he till with iron implements?'
'Yes'
'Does he make them himself?'
'No, he trades grain for them.'
'Trading grain for implements does not inflict hardship on the potters and founders. And when the potters and founders trade implements for grain, does this inflict hardship on the peasants? How can it be that Master Xu does not establish his own pottery and foundry? Why does he go about trading with the one hundred craftsmen? Why does he bother?'
   'The work of the one hundred craftsmen certainly cannot be done while tilling.'

If Mencius's thoughts were compiled in minus three hundred, they record a State in which iron implements were so common in China that they were regarded as necessary: but outside China they would be extremely uncommon everywhere.

Another assumption noted by Wagner is that the production of iron implements was a specialist craft which the peasant 'would be foolish to take up himself'.

Just as agriculture was transformed by iron, so was warfare. 'Iron tipped lances reached the enemy, and those without strong helmets and armour were injured.' While shields and bronze battle-axes were effective in ancient times, now they have been superseded by iron weapons and armour.

But the Qin did not necessarily prevail because of superiority in iron production. Here archaeological evidence is abundant, but rather difficult to interpret. Numerous graves have been excavated, uncovering many iron artefacts. The earlier graves have few such objects, but later there are many. However, the funerary traditions in the Qin Empire were different from those in the other Warring States, and the dearth of iron weapons in surviving Qin evidence may therefore lack significance.

Just as iron tools are not always better than bronze ones, bronze weapons can sometimes be more fit for purpose than iron ones. Crossbow locks were normally made of bronze, because these locks were precision mechanisms cast to very close tolerances, and 'bronze is far superior to iron in this sort of work'.

Considering the rise of the State of Qin, Wagner tells us:

'It is often suggested that the key to Qin's success lay in a technological superiority in weaponry, but real proof has never been forthcoming. Qin's first major conquest was in the southern state of Chu: if it is correct, ... that iron weapons were not used here, then this may be an example of a technological superiority contributing to Qin's success. (Definite proof that Qin's iron weapons were in fact superior to Chu's bronze weapons is still needed.) But Qin's further conquests cannot be explained in this way, for the evidence seems to be incontrovertible that iron had almost entirely replaced bronze for weapons throughout north China by the early decades of the -3rd century. If the hypothesis is to be saved, we must look rather to a superiority in the *organisation* of the production of iron weapons.

Weapons were made by smiths of wrought iron and steel. The technique of the smith is to a significant extent the same throughout the world and throughout history, and everywhere there are master smiths and incompetent smiths. We should therefore not expect to find much difference between Qin and the rest of north China in the smiths' actual techniques of production of weapons, but should look instead to the production of the smith's raw material. We know little about pre-Han primary iron-production techniques, but it seems likely that there was not much variation from place to place in ancient China: in iron production the most important variation was not in its underlying technique, but perhaps in its organisation. Production of iron in a blast furnace is most efficient at a high level of production, and mass production requires a large market, good transportation, and a large and reliable labour force. All these factors would be more easily forthcoming in the "totalitarian" state of Qin than in the more "feudal" states of north China. Qin's political practice and ideology made possible a reliable and efficient production of iron implements and weapons; this gave Qin an economic and military advantage over the other states; and this advantage made the Qin conquest possible.' (pages 146-7)

Wagner offers rich evidence from recent excavations which enables us to test the hypothesis of earlier scholars. It also enables us to identify questions which cannot at present be answered with any degree of certainty, and suggests important areas of further research.

In *The Grand Titration*, Needham discusses the influence of river controls and irrigation on the centralisation of power and authority in the Qin and later Empires. The water works transcended the barriers between separate territories of individual feudal or proto-feudal lords.

'It thus invariably tended to concentrate power at the centre, i.e., in the bureaucratic apparatus arched above the granular mass of "tribal" clan villages. I think it played an important part therefore in making Chinese feudalism "bureaucratic". Of course it does not matter from the standpoint of the historian of science and technology how different Chinese feudalism was from European feudalism, but it has got to be different enough (and I firmly believe that it was different enough) to account for the total inhibition of capitalism and modern science in China as against the successful development of both these features in the West.' (page 204)

Wagner's book has an awesome trajectory, from ancient China through the whole sweep of history. He generously records his debt to Needham, who laid the foundations for this phenomenal work, and had begun studying the history of ferrous metallurgy in China in the early 1950s. This has been an exemplary collaboration, building our knowledge and testing received wisdom in a continuously creative way.

Ken Coates

*   *   *

From the beginning the seventh volume of Needham's *History* was scheduled to be the last. In fact it split itself in two, and this second part, concluding the series, appeared in 2004. It is encouraging that it has already needed a reprint, just as we can draw encouragement that this final book is by no means the last, since intermediary volumes continue to emerge. The earlier books, much subdivided, continue to generate massive further contributions, and establish a veritable Needham industry. Needham told us that when a book was too bulky to read safely in the bath, then it must be split into its constituent parts. However, when the constituent parts themselves are too bulky to read in the bath, neither science nor civilisation has any easy remedy at hand.

Kenneth Robinson, who edited this last word, has put great love into it. We learn many things that not everyone will consider essential to its daunting subject, such as that Needham's mother composed the music for the anthem *Nelly Dean*, to whose strains some of us misspent our youth during too many closing time choruses. Or the quatrain we owe to Francesca Bray, the author of the section of Volume Six of the *History*, on Agriculture:

> *Dr Joseph Needham*
> *Dances with philosophic freedom*
> *You'd better watch your toes if*
> *You dance with Joseph*

Robinson tells us bluntly what is the agenda of this ultimate volume:

'we are most concerned ... with the great question of why modern science did not arise in China after so many centuries of technical leadership, and closely connected with this, why it was that modern capitalism did not develop in China.'

It was the effort to explain these matters that involved Needham in a study of the Asiatic Mode of Production, as set forth by Marx and Engels, and developed in the early works of Wittfogel in the German language. It also provoked the idea that historic China could be described as 'the prime example of "bureaucratic feudalism".' Needham recalls sitting with the Australian ambassador in a teahouse in Szechuan when the ambassador exclaimed how medieval everything was. 'You could almost expect to see a knight and men-at-arms come riding by.' Needham said 'yes' but 'it wouldn't have been a knight but rather a civilian official, and the men-at-arms would have been represented by unarmed servitors carrying his titles and dignities on placards'. Force was better concealed by Chinese bureaucrats.

This volume recapitulates many of the arguments first raised in *The Grand Titration*, and indeed whole chapters of that seminal work. True, it fails to close the file on the Needham question: but it does leave us with a sense of lively wonder, of awe at the power of the human mind. Mark Elvin, in his foreword, likens it to completing a reading of Gibbon's *Decline and Fall*. Yes, it is also a giant work of scholarship. But no, it is not a conclusion, but a prelude. Beyond this peak, new ridges shall arise.

KC

TomDispatch

Tom Engelhardt (editor), *The World According to TomDispatch: America in the New Age of Empire,* Verso, 346 pages, paperback ISBN 9781844672578, £10.99

This book grew out of internet exchanges between Tom Engelhardt, his friends, colleagues and acquaintances who wanted to rally dissident opinion on the foreign policy pursued by George W. Bush as President of the United States. The contributors are nearly all American, and all are extremely well-informed, including figures such as Noam Chomsky and Mike Davis. They provide a devastating home-grown critique of the US and its international relations under George W. Bush.

American policy is correctly described as imperialist. The 9/11 attacks on the Twin Towers gave the Bush entourage a pretext for launching their plans to implement the aims envisaged in the concept of the New American Century. After the fall of the Soviet Union, the so-called neo-cons around Bush argued that the US must do everything possible to prevent the development of rival power centres, whether friendly or hostile.

American efforts to offset China's growing importance to this end have included obstructing possible reunification with Taiwan, and efforts to use Japan as a surrogate counter-balance by reversing post-war US opposition to Japanese rearmament.

The United States has sought to retain its influence in Latin America, but elections have increasingly brought to power governments that are not only critical of unbridled capitalism, but have also insisted on pursuing independent policies. Colombian counter-insurgency operations continue to be supported in the hope of shoring up its position, but the US has been unsuccessful in its attempts to brand Venezuela under Chavez as a pariah state, and to limit his influence in the region as a whole.

United States policy has, above all, failed in the efforts expended to subdue Iraq and Afghanistan by force of arms. The book makes an irresistible case against the invasion of Iraq. Oil loomed large in its motivation, but the attempt to put oil reserves in the hands of the major international oil companies has encountered stiff resistance.

Paul Bremer, as head of the US occupation, instituted a flat tax, abolished tariffs, cancelled laws preventing foreign ownership of Iraqi companies, and permitted full repatriation of profits abroad. However, favoured American companies such as Halliburton and Bechtel – which were brought in as Republican cronies – have failed to restore the economy, despite making rich pickings, and resistance to western dominance remains.

The deaths of huge numbers of Iraqis, the flight abroad of three million refugees (12% of the population), the collapse of living standards, and the catastrophic deterioration of security are brought out in this book.

The damage done to Iraq's heritage as the location of early civilisations is said to be the worst since the Mongol conquest of 1258. Museums have been vandalised and looted, ancient books and documents have been destroyed by fire, military bases have been built adjacent to the remains of ancient cities, and unique sites have been wantonly disfigured or despoiled.

A statement issued by George W. Bush and Tony Blair in April 2003, which is quoted, reveals the huge gap between what was promised and what has been delivered:

> We reaffirm our commitment to protect Iraq's natural resources as the patrimony of the people of Iraq which should be used only for their benefit. [p. 107]

The decline in accepted standards of human rights is a feature of the administration. It includes the establishment of Guantanamo prison camp, the ill-treatment of prisoners at Abu Ghraib and other centres, the redefinition of torture to justify 'water-boarding' and other methods of causing pain to prisoners, and the practice of 'extraordinary rendition' of prisoners to countries where torture and ill-treatment are regularly inflicted on detainees.

Yet, despite all this and its huge military expenditure, the United States has been unable to subdue two underdeveloped countries. The book estimates that total Pentagon consumption of oil amounts to 340,000 barrels (four million gallons) every day [p. 215]. As one of the authors says, it would be both sad and ironic if the military began fighting wars mainly to guarantee its own fuel supplies.

The cost of all this has not been imposed on the wealthy. George W. Bush's tax cuts in 2003 gave $93,500 to every millionaire while the poor were bled by cuts in income and social benefits.

TomDispatch counterbalances the continual flood of biased information retailed by the western media to convince the public that the policies pursued by President George W. Bush and his allies are in their interests and promote democratic principles. The book is packed with facts and arguments which totally expose the destructive, pernicious and cruel consequences of United States policy as conducted by the present administration. It helps to explain how America's standing in many parts of the world has further plummeted in recent years, and emphasises that the present policies are inevitably destined to fail. That is one reason why a change of direction is vital.

Stan Newens

Contentious Figure

Wilfred Burchett, edited by George Burchett and Nick Shimmin, *Rebel Journalism: The Writings of Wilfred Burchett*, Forewords by John Pilger and Gavan McCormack, Cambridge University Press, 336 pages, paperback ISBN 9780521718264, £15.99

I suspect that the name of Wilfred Burchett may be unfamiliar to many *Spokesman* readers. I am not suggesting any blame on their part, but merely that Burchett's writings should be better known, and that his fellow countrymen should recognise and acknowledge his contribution. This can be achieved with the aid of this text, an anthology of his writings spanning his career as a journalist from the 1940s to the 1980s.

He published innumerable articles and more than 30 books. The writings included in this collection bring together most of the above, beginning with the Second World War, his acclaimed reports on Hiroshima following America dropping the atom bomb, Eastern Europe, Korea,

Russia, Laos, Cambodia, China, Vietnam, Angola, Zimbabwe and other areas from which Burchett reported.

Wilfred Burchett was born in Australia in 1911, and has been described as 'the greatest journalist and war correspondent Australia has ever produced'. Any fair-minded person would endorse this judgment, and yet he became, and sadly remains, a contentious figure. (The reviews of this text, when it was published in Australia in 2007, demonstrate that, in the eyes of right wing commentators, he merits the criticism and contumely which beset him throughout his life.)

Burchett's strength and the acclaim he has won relate to his independence for, unlike many journalists, he refused to toe any official or government line. The obsessive attitude of figures in the Australian establishment is vividly illustrated by an incident, in 1951, when he was visiting Melbourne to lecture. The Lord Mayor cancelled his lecture on world development, asserting that 'the letting of the town hall to a meeting in support of peace would be against the principles of the United Nations'. Later, when members of Burchett's family resided alongside Port Phillip Bay in Melbourne, government spies speculated that their choice might well have been motivated by a desire to communicate with 'the enemy' (by submarine!). Readers should not be surprised that the notorious Peter Wright chose to retire to Australia.

There are a number of matters which I suspect will be of interest to *Spokesman* readers. Burchett was the first Western reporter to visit Hiroshima after the atom bomb was dropped. He was warned by Japanese press officers that 'no one goes to Hiroshima: every one is dying there'. He slipped away from the press 'pack' and made his way to Hiroshima. The journey, mostly in darkness, is described. It demonstrates his courage. He travelled in a train packed with armed Japanese servicemen who, as one might have expected, were sullen and almost certainly bitter at the moment of their country's defeat. Burchett's report was widely circulated, and made the front page of the *Daily Express*. The headline is prescient: *I write this as a warning to the world.* Burchett reported, 'thirty days after the first atom bomb destroyed the city and shook the world, people are still dying mysteriously and horribly – people who were uninjured in the cataclysm – from an unknown something'. In comprehending and focusing on what he described as the 'atomic plague', he drew attention to the experimental nature of this, the first use of a nuclear weapon against a defenceless civil population. It is claimed, and no doubt correctly, that he was never forgiven for having given a truthful account of the destruction of Hiroshima, and the impact of atomic radiation. At the time, the American authorities sought to deny the truth of his reports, and the existence of the deadly radiation, which resulted in far more deaths than the impact of the explosion. 'It was a considerable ordeal to reach Hiroshima,' wrote the distinguished American journalist T. D. Allman when acknowledging Burchett's achievement, 'but it was an infinitely greater accomplishment, back then, to understand the importance of Hiroshima'.

I was also struck by Burchett's account of the American War in Vietnam, on which he reported extensively, and the recent references to the supposed heroism of McCain, and his conduct after being shot down over North Vietnam. Burchett records interviewing American prisoners of war who, much to their surprise, were well treated by their captors. He gives details of a conversation with an American Sergeant, who was injured when his base was attacked. Burchett reports him acknowledging that he was given immediate first aid when he was captured, and that the metal fragments resulting in his wounds were removed the day following. The Sgt. commented: 'They treated us real well – that's the main thing. No rough stuff of any kind. I never expected to be treated like that, a real surprise'. His report is revealing in pointing to the understanding of American servicemen as to the nature of the conflict, and the motivation displayed by Vietcong cadres whom he interviewed. He doesn't say so, but the conclusion is suggested by his report: American servicemen are 'thick' – obsessed with sport. He contrasts this with the realistic understanding of the Vietcong, and the sense of pride they must have felt in being Vietnamese. Having recently visited Vietnam, and seen the conditions under which they fought, I can attest this is no mere hyperbole.

Readers of my generation who lived through the American War in Vietnam and who cared about its outcome will have been struck by Burchett reporting a speech by the then Massachusetts Senator Kennedy, in 1954, when Vietnam was occupied by the French: 'To pour money, material and men into the jungle of Indochina without at least a remote prospect of victory would at least be dangerously futile and destructive … No amount of American assistance in Indochina can conquer an enemy which is everywhere, and at the same time nowhere, an "enemy of the people" which has the sympathy and support of the people'. I found this passage revealing, and it led me to speculate whether the conflict would have intensified to the point it developed under Johnson, had Kennedy lived.

No account of Burchett's life and work would be complete without reference to his courage and social commitment, which began in the 1930s when assisting Jews to escape from Nazi Germany. He did so at considerable risk to himself. His reward, an abiding shame along with much else on Australia's history, led to his losing his passport, and a refusal to allow him to visit and attend his father's funeral.

For seventeen years, Burchett and his children were denied passports by the Australian government. Despite their hostility, the government failed to bring any charge against him. The mean minded attitude of establishment figures is vividly expressed in a letter by a former Australian Prime Minister, Harold Holt. Writing in his capacity as Minister of Immigration, in 1965, he noted that Burchett 'left Australia fifteen years ago. He has not since returned, his wife is not an Australian … in addition his activities since his departure forfeited any claim he might have had to the protection he would receive as the holder of an Australian passport'.

Cambridge University Press, Burchett's son and his colleague are to be congratulated on the production of this volume. Anyone wishing to learn more of the history of the latter half of the last century would gain much from reading the thirty texts which make up the anthology.

Peter M. Jackson

No More Spin!

James Harding, *Alpha Dogs: The Americans Who Turned Political Spin Into a Global Business*, Atlantic Books, 384 pages, hardback ISBN 9781843548171, £22

I can well remember the early 1990s as a time of frantic political activity as the entire Eastern European state structures collapsed following the demolition of the Berlin Wall and the dissolution of the Soviet Union. As vice chair of the European Parliament's Delegation to South Eastern Europe, I was an observer at the elections in Albania, Bulgaria and Romania. We made several visits to these countries during the run up to their elections, mainly to contact the political groups and parties seeking to take part in the electoral contests.

As the elections drew closer, the increasing number of American accents, buzzing like bees around the various political and government offices, became more and more apparent to me. During the latter stages of the campaigns, and after the counts, it became clear that there was a pattern emerging from the contests both within and across the countries involved. I would not go as far as to say the whole thing had been scripted, but it did appear as if many of those directing events had met at their Alma Mater.

James Harding has to some extent provided an explanation for me in his book *Alpha Dogs* or *How Political Spin Became a Global Business*. In it he dwells on the rise and fall of an American company which dedicated itself to using new technologies to aid the campaigning of politicians and parties. It extended its techniques, which by then included the use of focus groups, to the commercial world. The book is all the better because the author takes time to round out the characters as if they were dramatis personae, as befits blurring the distinction between fact and fiction that is the stock in trade of the spin doctor. The tragic irony of it all lies in the ultimately worthless pursuit of populism. If everyone reads focus groups in the same manner, then what choice is there for the electorate? Instead of new technology and polling techniques encouraging people to go to the polls and make their free choice, we find that it is difficult to get more that half the population out to vote throughout the western world.

Through a narrative about running a single enterprise, Sawyer Miller, Harding helps to explain the way that the great American ideal of making the world a safe place for American capital is inserted, virus like, on a global stage. He also reveals the ability of companies such as Sawyer Miller to blow their own trumpets, and, indeed, for there employees to claim credit for popular uprisings such as Aquino's defeat of the appalling Marcos in the Philippines, as did Mark Malloch Brown, who was at this time a little known spin doctor. The techniques employed by this time had almost been routinised; keep the message simple, repeat it often, check how the focus groups are interpreting it, prepare material to go negative, and set up a network for polling day to give authenticity to claims of victory from your own exit poll. From The Philippines to Ukraine and Georgia we have seen the same pattern appearing. It is not surprising that Malloch Brown went on to serve George Soros, via his so called Open Society Institute, and, controversially, the Quantum Group of Funds.[1]

We do discover the occasional nugget. Regarding elections in the United Kingdom, for instance, one Joe Napolitan not only advised Marcos in The Phillipines, but also Neil Kinnock in 1992. His comment on the latter encounter was: 'we knew it was a hopeless cause'. The promiscuity of these

---

1 According to Wikipedia, 'The Quantum Group of Funds are privately owned hedge funds based on Curaçao (Netherlands Antilles) and Cayman Islands. They are currently advised by George Soros through his company Soros Fund Management. Soros started the fund in the early 1970s along with Jim Rogers. The shareholders of the funds are not publicly disclosed although it is known that the Rothschild family and other wealthy Europeans put $6 million into the funds in 1969. In 1992, the lead fund, Soros's Quantum Fund, became famous for 'breaking' the Bank of England, forcing it to devalue the pound. Soros had bet his entire fund in a short sale on the prediction that the British currency would drop in value. It did so, a coup that netted him a profit of $1 billion. In 1997, Soros was blamed for forcing sharp devaluations in Southeast Asian currencies.'

consultants knows no bounds. However, it was in their pursuit of the crock of gold that such great advisors to the rulers of the world came unstuck. Whilst so full of hubris that they felt able to advise on the running of states, they could not themselves run their own company, so that the collective mix of talents became self-destructive, and the leading lights went their own ways.

They have left a legacy, however, particularly in the use of high tech IT in elections, and the subsequent spiralling of costs of election campaigns. Instead of new technology opening up democracy to all the people, it has put the cost of entering the democratic process out of the reach of ordinary people. In the United States you need either to be a millionaire, or to be backed by one, to stand for any important election. The same has happened in the United Kingdom with Blair taking £1 million from Formula 1 motor racing, and European Union legislation on advertising tobacco being blocked in favour of F1. Separately, there has been the so-called 'cash for coronets' scandal concerning Labour Party funding. The introduction of focus groups has strapped the consultants across the input of campaign information, where they provide a subjective interpretation of unquantifiable data.

The importance of polling data is such that, in Nepal, a US group of political consultants who were trying to find out the views of villagers, sent a local pollster up in to the mountains. He was duly kidnapped by the Maoist rebels. As the poor wretch's luck would have it, the rebels sent a demand to yield up the polling data or the pollster gets it. They were given the findings, which appeared to satisfy all concerned, but not the raw data.

This is reminiscent of a struggle within the European Parliamentary Labour Party to get hold of polling data from the Shadow Communications Agency and its director, Philip Gould, that the EPLP had paid for. However, we didn't resort to kidnapping. And what happened to Malloch Brown? He's now Lord Malloch-Brown, one of Gordon Brown's Foreign Office ministers. No more spin, indeed!

Henry McCubbin

What about Israel?

Uri Avnery, edited by Sara R. Powell, *Israel's Vicious Circle: Ten Years of Writings on Israel and Palestine,* Pluto Press, 240 pages, hardback ISBN 9780745328232, £15.99

Uri Avnery is well known as a peace activist, and a courageous advocate of the rights of the Palestinian people. His time as a Member of Parliament brought him a wide audience, but he has been an unremitting campaigner inside or outside Parliament. For years he was the only MP demanding negotiations with the Palestinians, and he was the first Israeli to meet with Yasser Arafat.

His essays, sharp and always to the point, speak powerfully of the suppressed aspirations of Palestine. As he says, presently many leaders of the different factions in Palestine are in prison, from Marwan Barghouti, the leader of Fatah in the West Bank, to Sheik Abd-al-Khaliq Al-Natshe, a Hamas leader.

> 'With them there are leaders of Islamic Jihad, the Popular Front, and the Democratic Front. They spend their time there in permanent discussion, while keeping constant contact with the leaders of their organisations outside and the activists inside. God knows how they do it.'

As Avnery says, when the leaders of the prisoners speak with one voice, what they say carries a greater moral weight than the statements of any Palestinian institution, including the Presidency, the Parliament and the Government. That is why Avnery and his companions picketed the show trial of Marwan Barghouti carrying posters that said 'Send Barghouti to the negotiating table and not to prison!'

Mordantly, Avnery points out that the American invasion of Iraq to compel it to desist from the pursuit of nuclear weapons raises the question 'what about Israel?'

It was, of course, Mordechai Vanunu who told the *Sunday Times* about the Dimona nuclear weapons factory, and exposed the stockpiling of nuclear bombs by Israel. He was subsequently kidnapped, spirited away to Tel Aviv, and locked up for eighteen years, eleven of which he spent in solitary confinement. After he was 'liberated', ferocious restrictions were imposed on him. He could not leave Israel, could not leave one particular town, could not approach any Embassy or Consulate, and was forbidden to talk with foreign citizens.

Avnery points out that these rules had been imposed by the colonial British emergency regulations which had been denounced by the Jewish leaders in Palestine as 'worse than the Nazi laws'.

According to Avnery,

> 'In the short address Vanunu was able to make to the media immediately on his release, he made a strong remark: that the young woman who served as bait for his kidnapping, some eighteen years ago, was not a Mossad agent, as generally assumed, but an agent of the FBI or CIA. Why was it so urgent for him to convey this?

From the first moment, there was something odd about the Vanunu affair.

At the beginning, my first thought was that he was a Mossad agent. Everything pointed in that direction. How else can one explain a simple technician's success in smuggling a camera into the most secret and best-guarded installation in Israel? And in taking photos apparently without hindrance? How else to explain the career of that person who, as a student at Be'er-Sheva University, was well known as belonging to the extreme left and spending his time in the company of Arab fellow students? How was he allowed to leave the country with hundreds of photos? How was he able to approach a British paper and to turn over to British scientists material that convinced them that Israel had 200 nuclear bombs?

Absurd, isn't it? But it all fits, if one assumes that Vanunu acted from the beginning on a mission for the Mossad. His disclosures in the British newspaper not only caused no damage to the Israeli government, but on the contrary, strengthened the Israeli deterrent without committing the government, which was free to deny everything.

What happened next only reinforced this assumption. While in London, in the middle of his campaign of exposures, knowing that half a dozen intelligence services are tracking his every movement, he starts an affair with a strange woman, is seduced into following her to Rome, where he is kidnapped and shipped back to Israel. How naïve can you get? Is it credible for a reasonable person to fall into such a primitive trap? It is not. Meaning that the whole affair was nothing but a classic cover story.

But when the affair went on, and details of the years-long daily mistreatment of the man became public, I had to give up this initial theory. I had to face the fact that our security services are even more stupid than I had assumed (which I wouldn't have believed possible) and that all these things actually had happened, and that Mordecai Vanunu was an honest and idealistic, if extremely naïve, person.

I have no doubt that his personality was shaped by his background. He is the son of a family with many children, who were quite well-to-do in Morocco but lived in a primitive 'transition camp' in Israel before moving to Be'er-Sheva, where they lived in poverty. In spite of this, he succeeded in getting into university and got a Master's degree, quite an achievement, but suffered, so it seems, from the overbearing attitude and prejudices of his Ashkenazi peers. Undoubtedly, that pushed him towards the company of the extreme left, where such prejudices were not prevalent.

The bunch of 'security correspondents' and other commentators who are attached to the udders of the security establishment have already spread stories about Vanunu 'imagining things', his long stay in solitary confinement causing him to 'convince himself of all kinds of fantasies' and to 'invent all kinds of fabrications'. Meaning: the American connection.

Against this background one can suddenly understand all these severe restrictions, which, at first sight, look absolutely idiotic. The Americans, it seems, are very worried. The Israeli security services have to dance to their tune. The world must be prevented by all available means from hearing, from the lips of a credible witness, that the Americans are full partners in Israel's nuclear arms program, while pretending to be the world's sheriff for the prevention of nuclear proliferation.'

A strange accusation! How far is it true? Had it been made by anybody but Avnery, we would have ignored it. But since he has made it, we owe it to him to publish, and invite responses.

James Jones

Forgotten Democracy

David Roberts, *The European Union and You: Understanding the Constitution, the Reform Treaty and the Arguments*, Saxon Books, 600 pages, hardback ISBN 9780952896944, £24.99

Jan Orbie, *Europe's Global Role: External Policies of the European Union*, Ashgate, 232 pages, hardback ISBN 9780754672203, £55

June 2009 will see the seventh European Union General Election to the European Parliament taking place. If this had been on the timescale of an American Presidential election, our British media would have already subjected us to at least a year of party politics and primaries, and even those who had failed to reach nomination would have become familiar names to the British populace. I doubt if you could find more than a handful of people in the streets here who could tell you when the next European Parliamentary elections take place, let alone name anyone taking part. Although Kilroy Silk's appearance on 'I'm a celebrity' might just prove me wrong.

As someone who has actively participated in European politics, I can only express my exasperation at the disinterested attitude of the media in the United Kingdom, encouraged, I believe, by the major political parties, towards this important political event. With half the resources spent by the BBC on its coverage of the US elections, it could quite easily raise the awareness of our public to the importance of these elections to British citizens who, unlike with the US elections, actually have a vote which can register change in the make up of the European Parliament. It is ironic that it is in Scotland, the part of the United Kingdom in which independence from the UK, but continued EU membership, is actively being discussed, the BBC produces a programme in Gaelic (with English subtitles) called Eòrpa (Europe), which covers European political, economic, cultural and social affairs. This is the only such main channel programme transmitted in the United Kingdom.

It is not as if information on the topic is in itself hard to come by. The European Union institutions have extensive web sites, as have the political Groups within the European Parliament, often covering the issues in real time. Although the very designation 'group' indicates that these political formations are not 'parties', a title which bestows greater authority. The problem with coverage as it is now presented is that the European Union is portrayed as a series of unconnected events, instead of the political process that it undoubtedly is. Hence, the appearance that new EU legislation drops, as if from outer space, on the laps of unprepared editors. A recent case in point is the working time directive where the supine Labour MEPs broke with the habit of a lifetime and actually voted with the majority in Parliament to force the UK Government into line. This was a major breach in discipline, but received no more than a couple of paragraphs in the broadsheets.

Coming up over the next few months will be the Irish government's response to its people voting against the Lisbon Treaty. I would conjecture that an attempt will be made to tie support for the euro based Irish banks to a Yes vote. Will this impact on the UK? It probably will in that it may remind people that we are, after all, members of the European Union, and that Gordon Brown declared five tests for the UK economy before we could join the euro. The first test concerns whether the UK has achieved 'convergence' with the rest of the European Union. You could certainly posit that our economic cycles were in step as we all descend, like Olympic synchronised divers, into recession; the second, whether there is sufficient economic flexibility in the UK and the EU to avoid problems: with a reserve army of unemployed being created at speed, this test also gets a tick against it; the third test concerns the effects on inward investment; there is hardly any competition for this at this moment as there is none; the fourth test affects those in the City of London, no doubt so busy fearing the EU that they were completely unsighted on the great trough of sub-prime junk IOUs across the Atlantic. Finally, the Chancellor and his economic advisers listed as the 'fifth test' for Britain's entry into the euro the general economic effects of monetary union on the British economy, thus exposing the whole sham as a political exercise all along.

With six months to go until the next European Elections, there has been the recent publication of two relevant books. The first, *The European Union and You* by David Roberts, which provides a helpful collection of current issues and recent legislation which should form the basis for the political arguments through to next spring. The second is *Europe's Global Role*, edited by Jan Orbie, which covers an aspect of the European Union obscured even more by the member state politicians than issues of sovereignty. As the European Union's importance as a major trader and the home of a major currency grows, the perceived need for co-operation in external affairs, including that of the national militaries, has captured more European Council time and security organisation resources. This has been a highly contentious issue, which the major actors have done their utmost to keep behind closed doors, and assign to obscure committees with acronyms or apparently unrelated geographical titles. The whole objective with Europe's near neighbours has been to 'marketise' their economies, which may in hindsight now look like a wasteful exercise for all concerned. These two books illuminate how this neoliberal drift happened. Why it was allowed to happen will probably be revealed as our media steadfastly looks across the Atlantic, with its back to where the relevant action now is.

Henry McCubbin

Viva Cuba!

Dervla Murphy, *The Island that Dared,* Eland Publishing, 320 pages, hardback ISBN 9781906011352, £16.99

This is a remarkable book by a remarkable woman. Undoubtedly, already well known to the aficionados of travel writing, Dervla Murphy had to defer her back-packing wanderings to her later years, owing to early family caring responsibilities, but by her early 70s had managed to travel extensively. Her travels now encompass Tibet, India, Ethiopia, Afghanistan, Madagascar, Southern Africa, the Balkans, Siberia and much of South America. She has written more than 20 titles (her first book dates from 1965, *Ireland to India With a Bicycle*) and was still considering a cycling excursion in Ussuriland in eastern Russia at 71 when a broken knee intervened. As one can see, we are dealing with an intrepid traveller! This book follows her three visits to Cuba in 2005, 2006 and 2007 respectively, firstly with her daughter and three grandchildren, but the latter two by herself.

The book is much more, however, than a travel book, largely eschewing tourist Cuba, in favour of city backwaters, rural areas and towns, but it does contain helpful hints, not least of which is to be aware of the discomforts of train travel in Cuba. The writer is well aware that Cuba, emerging from the 'Special Period', is embracing a new reality fraught with both dangers and opportunities. She makes the contradictions of the present vividly stark: an impoverished economy with a virtually skeletal transport system; inadequate housing, much of it in disrepair; overly bureaucratic administration teetering over into petty corruption. Over the years the American blockade and the Soviet abandonment have exacted a dreadful price. And yet, the revolution has delivered a largely caring people, vibrant without the obvious acquisitive attributes of western societies, with an 'idea of equality . . . who never felt inferior' because they lacked the western world's 'goodies'. The author contrasts this with the 'hungry, ragged, dirty or obviously diseased' she has encountered throughout her travels in the Third World. It is a fact, of course, that Cuba's health system is equal to that of many western countries, and its health education programme has facilitated the export of Cuban doctors throughout the Third World. Fidel has obviously strong feelings about 'graduating as a doctor' as one of the 'noblest actions a human being can do for others', and this ethos has obviously been imparted successfully to the temporary Cuban medical volunteers, few of whom are tempted to lucrative positions in western medicine when being abroad makes this a possibility. The author can boast unwelcome personal experience of the efficacy of Cuban health resources, when she collapsed into delirium with acute sunstroke (*hyperpyrexia*) in a remote Cuban town. She was treated by a local Cuban doctor who arrived within 15 minutes by bicycle.

The author obviously has the personality and the easy humanity to engage with other people, whatever the language or cultural impediments. As a result the book is able to give insight into the thinking of a wide cross-section of Cuban society. These range from the committed *Fidelista* to the disenchanted exiles of Miami, and she made a point of seeking out the views, within Cuba itself, of known dissidents. The book therefore gives a clear indication of the majority bedrock support for the revolution amongst the Cuban population, but this is accompanied by, unfortunately, a relatively extensive disenchantment among many of the young, together with a more generalised irritation with many of the bureaucratic regulations governing some aspects of Cuban society.

The book is a mine of information on Cuban history and the island's difficulties with its overbearing neighbour to the north, all contextually linked within the narrative of the travelogue. The author visits the Santa

Clara memorial to Ché, Playa Giron (the Bay of Pigs) and Fidel's birthplace, as well as wandering through the battlefields of the revolutionary war in the Sierra Maestra. One poignant reminder of this war is mentioned when the author meets an 80 year-old wheelchair veteran of the rebel army in the small town of Manzanillo, who during the uprising remembers twice covertly fetching Ché's asthma medicine from the local doctor's daughter. This day of discussion was the occasion of perhaps too many Buccaneros (Cuban beer) and too much sun resulting in, as mentioned above, the need for speedy medical attention!

The book is short on hard economic facts (a travel book is perhaps not quite the right vehicle anyway), but there is some discussion of Cuban agriculture and the turn away from the approach of Soviet agriculture, led initially by Fidel. This is before the Soviet collapse and the commencement of the Special Period. Cuba was to move subsequently to a more balanced, ecologically-guided farming including the adoption of town allotments on a mass scale, using often previously derelict land. Cuba is highly dependent on food imports, a situation she is striving to combat. The present economic climate has been greatly helped by the support of Chavez and, in particular, Venezuelan oil, and hopefully to be further aided by the discovery, recently, of large oil deposits off the coast of Cuba, thus easing the island's dependency on tourism.

The final part of the book is taken up with observations about Cuba's central dilemma: namely the rate and form of its accommodation with the Market, and the political and economic changes this may engender. As to the democratic nature of Cuban society, the book has some detailed reflections on the positive aspects of local municipal elections, and places democracy at the national level in the context of South American attitudes to revolution, differing as it does from western conceptions of revolutionary violence. Certainly, Cuba still needs to be able to defend herself against the economic blockade and the machinations of violent exile groups payrolled by the CIA/FBI. In fact the book mentions the many assassination attempts, terrorist activities and infiltrations, ceaseless negative propaganda and defamation, even the possible use of biological warfare, all directed against Cuba. The sense of siege hardly assists the democratic process.

Having said all this, it would be timely to note the words of the Cuban philosopher and polymath Antonio Blanco: 'If it is possible to "reinvent" socialism anywhere, then the conditions for doing so exist on this island'.

The Island that Dared is a truly Caribbean treasure trove, successful at every level: from feeling the pulse of the Cuban psyche, to understanding the everyday problems confronted by its ordinary citizens, to learning about Cuba's history, appreciating the political and economic problems it faces and, as a tourist guide, to getting around the country (not an easy business) and seeing some of the sights. Dervla Murphy's book is a magnificent act of solidarity with a country threatened by powerful outside forces, which would very much like to see the final snuffing out of any lingering alternative to globalised capitalism. Let us hope they are unsuccessful!

John Daniels

On Bardsey Island

Fflur Dafydd, *Twenty Thousand Saints*, Alcemi, 252 pages, paperback, ISBN 9780955527227, £9.99

Bardsey Island (Ynys Enlli) lies about two miles off the tip of the Llŷn Peninsula in North Wales. Day-trippers are welcome during the summer months, but are warned to be careful, as islands can be dangerous. So says the official Bardsey website, and the warning is echoed by Fflur Dafydd in her beautifully composed novel, *Twenty Thousand Saints*.

It is summer and the Island has opened itself up to visitors once more. The first to arrive is a filmmaker, Leri, and her companion Greta. Next is Mererid, the writer-in-residence, who, after missing the early morning boat, finally makes it ashore. The last to appear is the sinister Iestyn. Already living on Bardsey are a silent nun, Sister Vivian, a forlorn archaeologist named Deian, and Elin, a sensual woman whom all seem to admire. Accompanying each of them are their secrets – their darkest secrets, which the Island itself intends to out.

Mischief and madness are found in all the places on the small, secluded Bardsey Island of this novel. Fflur Dafydd's poetic narrative breathes life into her carefully constructed characters. Each one of them shares all with the reader, but nothing with each other, reflecting both the vast expanse of nature, and their compact community on Bardsey. They all have their own space, but each is confined.

Although a little slow in picking up momentum, Dafydd's story unearths each character's hidden secret, and compels the reader to dig deeper. *Twenty Thousands Saints* is a dark, comedic thriller that explores intense bonds between people and their loved ones. It is a gripping read.

Abi Rhodes

THE BERTRAND RUSSELL PEACE FOUNDATION
DOSSIER

2009   Number 29

FALSE ACCUSATIONS AGAINST RUSSIA

'On 15 August 2008, Human Rights Watch (HRW) accused the Russian Federation of having used cluster bombs in the conflict with Georgia. These accusations were widely repeated in the "western" media. The Russian Federation consistently denied any use of cluster ammunition. As it now turns out, the repeated accusations were wrong. The "evidence" provided by Human Rights Watch was based on pictures and mis-identified ammunition in those.

The ammunition in question is of Israeli origin and was used by the Georgian military. The Georgian Ministry of Defence has now admitted as much. Human Rights Watch has now also acknowledged this in a press statement. But it continues to claim Russian use of such weapons. It does so by pointing to its own older reports which clearly misidentified Georgian cluster ammunition as Russian made ...

While reviewing the story as documented below, notice the special role of Human Rights Watch's "senior military analyst" Marc Garlasco in this propaganda effort. An August 15 HRW press release claimed:

> Human Rights Watch said Russian aircraft dropped RBK-250 cluster bombs, each containing 30 PTAB 2.5M submunitions, on the town of Ruisi in the Kareli district of Georgia on August 12, 2008. On the same day, a cluster strike in the center of the town of Gori killed at least eight civilians and injured dozens, Human Rights Watch said.

In that press release and on its website Human Rights Watch provided a picture as evidence identifying the weapon debris shown as a Russian RBK-250 clusterbomb. But a zoomed picture of the "bomb" shows that the fins of this object are cambered. Cambered fins are typical for tube-launched missiles. While in the tube, the fins are wrapped around the missile body. When leaving the tube, the spring-loaded fins snap into their flight position but keep their original curved surface. In contrast, air dropped 'dumb' bombs such as the RBK-250 have straight fixed fins ... Note also that the diameter of an RBK-250 is 325 mm. The debris picture shown by Human Rights Watch and the object identified as RBK-250 only has roughly half that diameter. The Human Rights Watch expert quoted with the wrong identifications is one Marc Garlasco:

> "Cluster bombs are indiscriminate killers that most nations have agreed to outlaw," said Marc Garlasco, senior military analyst at Human Rights Watch. "Russia's use of this weapon is not only deadly to civilians, but also an insult to international efforts to avoid a global humanitarian disaster of the kind caused by landmines."

One wonders how Human Rights Watch and Marc Garlasco, its senior military analyst quoted in the report, missed those obvious inconsistencies in their "evidence" when making their accusations.

In its second report of 21 August 2008, Human Rights Watch showed pictures from alleged Russian sub-ammunition on Georgian ground:

> Human Rights Watch researchers saw and photographed unexploded submunitions from cluster munitions in and around the villages of Shindisi, in the Gori district of Georgia …
>
> "Many people have died because of Russia's use of cluster munitions in Georgia, even as Moscow denied it had used this barbaric weapon," said Marc Garlasco, senior military analyst at Human Rights Watch. "Many more people could be killed or wounded unless Russia allows professional demining organizations to enter at once to clean the affected areas."

This second report contains pictures of unexploded submunitions as evidence. A Human Rights Watch chart identifies an M85 submunition as produced by various "western" countries. The bomblet in the picture is identified as PTAB 2.5M, content of the Russian RBK-250 clusterbombs. It is obvious that the pictures from Georgia resemble the western submunitions type. Pictures from the 2006 Lebanon war show similar M85 submunitions dropped by Israel. Again one has to ask why Human Rights Watch senior military analyst Marc Garlasco mis-identifies these.

The government of Georgia has admitted that it used cluster ammunition in the recent war. It did so after a request from a different Human Rights Watch expert:

> The Georgian MoD released a press statement on Monday evening after Human Rights Watch (HRW) said on September 1 that in a letter sent to HRW, the Georgian side had admitted to using cluster bombs in the vicinity of Roki Tunnel, linking breakaway South Ossetia with Russia.
>
> "The Georgian armed forces have GRADLAR 160 multiple launch rocket systems and MK4 LAR 160 type (with M85 bomblets) rockets with a range of 45 kilometers," the Georgian MoD said.

The GRADLAR 160 is a product of the Israel Military Industry Ltd. It uses tube-launched missiles with a diameter of 160mm and M85 submunition. It seems that a different researcher than Marc Garlasco at Human Rights Watch finally made a correct identification and contacted the Georgians:

> Bonnie Docherty, arms division researcher at HRW, said on September 1 that M85 cluster munitions were discovered in Shindisi, a village outside breakaway South Ossetia, north of the town of Gori. Docherty said that while this could point to Russian use, Moscow was not known to have that particular make in its arsenal. She added that it was possible that the M85 munitions had been scattered about, having been hit in a Russian strike.

It is also possible, and much more likely, that Georgian troops fired their cluster-ammunition rockets against advancing Russian troops in Shindisi, i.e. on Georgian native ground, hitting their own population. A Russian strike on a Georgian GRADLAR launcher would certainly not have 'scattered' such ammunition intact …

Despite the new finding that submunitions found in Shindisi are not of Russian origin, Human Rights Watch in its 1 September press release still speaks of Russian cluster bomb usage:

> Human Rights Watch said it welcomed Georgia's willingness to acknowledge its use of cluster munitions and expressed hope that this was a first step toward adopting the treaty …
>
> In August, Human Rights Watch documented Russia's use of several types of cluster munitions, both air- and ground-launched, in a number of locations in Georgia's Gori district, causing 11 civilian deaths and wounding dozens more (http://hrw.org/english/docs/2008/08/20/georgi19660.htm). Russia continues to deny using cluster munitions.
>
> "Russia has yet to own up to using cluster munitions and the resulting civilian casualties," said Garlasco.

But all Human Rights Watch 'documented' in its earlier reports was misidentified debris and submunition. On what basis, then, is Marc Garlasco again making these accusations when the only proof for them are the August 15 and August 21 HRW reports which mistakenly identify Israeli made rockets and submunitions as Russian? …

If Human Rights Watch wants to achieve a somewhat believable, neutral position in conflicts, it would be well advised to distance itself from a 'senior military analyst' who is not able to distinguish 160 mm tube launched rockets from 325 mm airdrop bombs and uses such false 'evidence' for partisan accusation.

We again point to the professional history of Marc Garlasco and question his suitability for his current "human rights" job:

"Before coming to HRW, Marc spent seven years in the Pentagon as a senior intelligence analyst covering Iraq. His last position there was chief of high-value targeting during the Iraq War in 2003. Marc was on the Operation Desert Fox (Iraq) Battle Damage Assessment team in 1998, led a Pentagon Battle Damage Assessment team to Kosovo in 1999, and recommended thousands of aim points on hundreds of targets during operations in Iraq and Serbia. He also participated in over 50 interrogations as a subject matter expert".'

Source: www.moonofalabama.org, 2 September 2008

A COMMUNICATION FROM HONDURAS

Long-time Spokesman subscriber Nigel J. Potter writes:

You should take a look at Honduran politics. Honduras boasts the third biggest American Embassy in the world (after Iraq and Israel). Why should a little, third world, undeveloped banana republic like Honduras (I use such terms on purpose) have a modern, state-of-the-art fortress on its land? ... Well, of course, because the US was waging war in Nicaragua (with the Contras), in El Salvador (against the FMLN) and Guatemala, and basically dominating the whole continent. It is not without cause that Honduras has been nicknamed 'USS Honduras'.

Mel Zelaya is the first President and politician who, in the 18 years I have been here, has caught my attention. He can't pay his teachers (which is why they are always on strike) and health services are abysmal, but he has actually given the finger to the gringos. He goes to Cuba, invites to visit and meets up with Hugo Chavez, Evo Morales and Ortega. He openly denounces capitalism and berates the United States for its coups in Latin American countries. Furthermore, he advocates the legalisation of drugs, given the disastrous 'war on drugs' (did no one learn the lessons of the Volstead Act and prohibition?).

The press is up in arms against Zelaya because this 'free' press is run by local élites who all have interests in the US. What amazes me is that Zelaya, one of the élite, dare say such things. Where is his support coming from? Perhaps Mel Zelaya is just more geared up than the rest. Just another opportunistic politician (why should he be different from the rest?). He realises there are cracks fast appearing in the American Empire. The collapse of said Empire may takes us all with it, but it is collapsing, especially in Latin America, given the USA's obsession with Iraq, Iran and Afghanistan.

Bakers, Food & Allied Workers Union

Supporting workers in struggle
Wherever they may be.

Joe Marino   General Secretary
Ronnie Draper   President
Jackie Barnwell   Vice President

Stanborough House,
Great North Road,
Stanborough,
Welwyn Garden City,
Hertfordshire. AL8 7TA

Phone 01707 260150 & 01707 259450
www.bfawu.org

Making a difference
for shipbreakers and related industries in India

GMB MAKING A DIFFERENCE

GMB is working with the Mumbai Port Trust Dock and General Employees Union (MPTDGEU) in India, to create better conditions for metalworkers in shipbreaking and related industries in Mumbai and Alang in India.

NO RIGHTS
The workers toil all day for the equivalent of 50 pence. Conditions are the worst you can imagine – but as the workers themselves say, 'exploitation is better than starvation'.

There is a near absence of protective clothing and workers are often forced to work barefoot. They work with corrosive chemicals, asbestos and flammable and explosive toxins which are often outlawed in the West. They operate dangerous machinery; carry heavy loads with no basic heath and safety. They are burnt, cut, bruised, blinded, there is loss of limbs, often injuries are fatal, there are no hospitals nearby and no compensation.

Home is often a mere piece of tarpaulin secured with string and stones, with no running water or access to sanitation. There are no schools, no electricity, no running water and no sanitation.

MAKING A DIFFERENCE
The MPTDGEU, formed in 1920, has a history of organising. It has already had successes in providing benefits for workers in shipbreaking – providing drinkable water and creating the first shipbreakers' union. GMB is involved in developing a project which will see the unionisation and organising of metal workers in the industry, bringing an end to this brutal form of exploitation masquerading as 'globalisation'.

JOIN WITH GMB AND MAKE A DIFFERENCE
You can make a donation which will go directly to benefit the members of our sister union the MPTDGEU, or you can specifically sponsor one of the following items – large or small, everything helps.

The office of the MPTDGEU – The Workers House – is at the very heart of the community. It provides free space to a local primary school, there is a school for the children of shipbreakers, educational programmes for workers and women, health programmes, and political and social meetings take place here.

SCHOOL
A bare room with 30 children who sit on rush mats. They need everything.
- Teacher's salary (per month) **£120**
- Whiteboard, pens and duster **£12**
- Text books, standard level 1 to 4 (£12 x 30) **£360***
- Text books, standard level 5 to 10 (£15 x 30) **£450***
- Note books (per hundred) **£15**
- Ball point pens (per hundred) **£4**
- Pencils (per hundred) **£3**
- Story books **£1**
- Equipment, erasers, sharpeners, compass (per child) **£1.20**

*These books can be used for years

OLDER PEOPLE
- Medicines/operations **£10** to **£30**
- Umbrellas **£1**
- Zimmer **£8.50**
- Tricycle **£60**
- Ex gratia pension to those with no income and no person earning in the family (per month) **£18**

ANTI ASBESTOS CAMPAIGN
- 2,000 T-shirts including printing costs **£1,600**
- Banner for anti asbestos campaign **£15**
- Placards **£100**

COMMUNICATION
- Purchase of radio/megaphone **£60**
- Film projector **£720**
- Computer **£600**

RECRUITMENT OFFICER
- Sponsor a worker for a year **£2,000**

SEWING PROJECT
- Purchase of three sewing machines (each) **£300**
- Part-time tutor (per year) **£850**

MOTORCYCLE
The workplaces on Alang beach are spread over 10 kilometres of rough terrain, with no roads and no public transport. A motorcycle is vital to recruit and organise in this area. At a cost of **£700**

YES, I WANT TO MAKE A DIFFERENCE

GMB branch and region ....

Address ....

Telephone .... Email ....

Donation ....

Towards ....

Or the general fund..

Please make cheques payable to GMB/Shipbreaking and send with this form to Joni McDougall, GMB, 22/24 Worple Road, London SW19 4DD

If you would like further information on GMB's work or if you would like a speaker to address your branch meeting please contact Joni at the address above, or on 020 8971 4272 or joni.mcdougall@gmb.org.uk